The Preceptor's Handbook

Charles J Carter

LEWIS MASONIC
Books

By the same author
   The Director of Ceremonies
   The Inner Guard and Deacons
   The Lodge Secretary
   The Lodge Almoner

First published in England 1994
by Lewis Masonic, Ian Allan Regalia Ltd
Coombelands House, Coombelands Lane
Addlestone, Surrey KT15 1HY,
who are members of the Ian Allan Group

ISBN 085318 2019

British Library Cataloguing in Publication Data.

A Catalogue record for this book is available from the British Library

Printed in Great Britain by
Latimer Trend & Company Ltd, Plymouth, Devon

Contents

About The Author

Charles James Carter was initiated into the Three Pillars Lodge No 4923 in May 1962, became Master in 1971 and Secretary the following year. In 1971 he became Founding Secretary of the Plantagenets Lodge No 8409 in the Province of Kent and Master in 1973. He served the office of Preceptor and Director of Ceremonies for ten years.

In 1977 he was promoted to Provincial Deputy Grand Director of Ceremonies, a rank he was to hold for ten years before being promoted to Assistant Provincial Grand Master (West Kent) in 1987.

His memberships have included many Lodges and Chapters in London and Kent including the West Kent Provincial Grand Stewards' Lodge No 8565 and West Kent Masters' Lodge No 5778, in each of which he occupied the role of Director of Ceremonies for eight years. He is an Honorary member of thirty-four Lodges and sixteen Chapters.

He was appointed to the rank of Past Assistant Grand Director of Ceremonies in 1981 and promoted to Past Senior Grand Deacon in 1988. In the Royal Arch he was appointed to the rank of Past Grand Standard Bearer in 1985.

He is the current secretary of the Quatuor Coronati Correspondence Circle Limited, London, where he is responsible for the worldwide operations of the Correspondence Circle of the Quatuor Coronati Lodge, the Premier Lodge of Masonic Research in the world to which he was elected a full member in 1992.

Chapter 1:

Introduction

For the majority of newly-made freemasons the first introduction both to the word and to the person of a Preceptor of a Lodge of Instruction comes shortly after their Initiation.

It is not at all unusual for the mind of a newly-initiated candidate to be full of questions which, when mixed together with a liberal amount of doubt as to the correctness or not of asking for answers, places our recently-made brother in a quandary.

Let us recount his masonic experiences so far. They have been those of being interviewed prior to admission, subsequently told he was acceptable and would in due time be initiated. He was then given a date and time to attend for his initiation together with instructions on what he should wear and what he would be required to pay either before or on the night of the ceremony.

His subsequent experience was that of being blindfolded, then being told precisely what to do and when to do it. Surely it was now reasonable for him to expect that someone would tell him what he needed to know when they thought it was appropriate and that the asking of questions was to say the least, highly inappropriate for he did not wish to seem brash, forward or lacking in good manners now that he was a member (albeit quite inexperienced) of this new brotherhood.

Most brethren will find it hard to remember with crystal clarity the feelings they experienced on the night of their initiation, but for those who can they will recall that the evening was filled with a mixture of understandable apprehension, awe, surprise, relief and even a mild amount of fear and concern for what lay ahead—we could call it the fear of the unknown.

Suddenly our newly-made brother is invited to attend his first Lodge of Instruction—what is this strange sounding occasion? He may well have been told by his proposer that it is where rehearsals take place for the ceremony he experienced so recently.

The first thing he notices is the distinct informality of the Lodge of Instruction compared with the formal atmosphere of the Lodge meeting itself. The brethren are casually dressed, some coming from their place of work and others, perhaps the older members who are retired, from their homes. He is welcomed and quickly finds that he is known to everyone but of course has the disadvantage of knowing the names of hardly anyone at all except perhaps his proposer and seconder.

The scenario given above is to try and set the scene for the budding new Preceptor or to remind the Preceptor of many years standing who has perhaps forgotten, the feelings he experienced when he was the newest member and just what this first attendance of the LOI can mean to a totally inexperienced and perhaps mildly insecure brother.

If this first visit is not handled with great care and preconceived thought it can have the totally wrong effect on the newly-made brother. It might well frighten him into believing that to perform such work (ritual) entirely from memory is quite outside his capability, and furthermore something he would not be prepared even to consider tackling.

This book has been compiled with the training of new and inexperienced freemasons totally in mind. The art, for that is what it is, in taking newly-made freemasons and creating competent understanding and useful lodge officers is a task for which few are prepared when they are asked to accept the role of Preceptor.

The chapters which follow have been prepared individually to allow for specific types of problems to be identified. All members of the lodge have their individual strengths and weaknesses. It is knowing and understanding the differences and thereby being able to support the weaknesses and build on the strengths which separate the outstanding Preceptor from his run of the mill counterpart.

The author hopes that this book will prove of assistance to the reader in the tasks which lie ahead of him in his new role and that when the time arrives for him to lay down his mantle of office, those years of dedication to his lodge will allow him to enjoy the happiest of memories of a job well done and a plethora of competent lodge officers as well as Past Masters as the outward sign of his handiwork.

Chapter 2:

Why Preceptor?

The word Preceptor takes its origin from the base word 'precept' which of course stands for 'a rule for conduct', 'a maxim', 'an instruction' or 'a rule' depending upon the dictionary chosen. The word Preceptor therefore exists to categorize the person who explains and teaches those same 'rules for conduct', 'maxims', or instructions. It may interest you to know that the word 'preceptress' also exists and of course means the female equivalent of the former.

Now that we have established the meaning of the word let us turn to the person to whom it is applied for he, in the same manner as our teacher at school, is charged with the difficult task of imparting knowledge to as wide a selection of individuals as can be imagined. Each of them has his own speed of learning and, equally, each has his own level of determination to succeed or not depending upon his interest in that which he has experienced thus far, or perhaps on his enthusiasm to find out more about this very different organization of which he has but only recently become a member.

Why should any brother wish to accept this ongoing role which demands (for many) a regular weekly commitment to attend a place of tuition throughout the coldest months of the year?

Surely trying to teach anyone anything at the end of the working day when tiredness is maximized must be the worst possible time, both to impart and expect retention of, facts, instruction and explanations.

Perhaps the answer to this lies in the simple but true fact that a successful Lodge of Instruction is much more than a simple 'learning academy'. It is a venue for friends to meet each other, to offer encouragement and enthusiasm as the younger members, masonic-ally speaking, rehearse their expertise.

They will have the benefit of knowing that everyone who has gone before them has experienced the same highs and lows as they have. It was either a good evening or one which did not live up to their expectations for, at the end of the day, it is a brother's view of his own performance which pleases or displeases him, not what the brethren said to him about his work that evening.

Learning anything is a process in which every individual differs from his neighbour. We all know of those fortunate individuals who can look at a page of typescript once and have the rudiments of its meaning clearly engraved on their minds within quite a short time.

We equally know of brethren who try very hard over so many years but whose powers of retention leave them high and dry just when they need help the most.

Such my brother is but an indication of the most basic requirements needed in a Preceptor to enable him to handle both types of situation. To support strengths and encourage and enthuse those who show weakness must surely be amongst the most basic tenets of Freemasonry.

Chapter 3:

Explaining the LOI to a New Member

A newly initiated brother will have heard within the general chatter which abounds amongst members of the craft about this strange entity called the 'Lodge of Instruction' which, depending upon the imagination of the individual, can range in his mind from a school-room of his childhood to some sort of space-age infusion of knowledge directly into his brain.

The necessity therefore to impart accurate meaningful information to potential new members is vital if we are not to transmit to such brethren a whole range of fears and apprehensions related to expectation, involvement, attendance and financial commitment.

It is always better for the Preceptor of the Lodge of Instruction to make the first approach to the new member well before that member attends the LOI for the first time and ideally a face to face approach would be the best way in which to handle this situation. Sometimes, however, it is not possible to achieve the right moment within the ambiance of the after proceedings of the lodge meeting and therefore this has to be accomplished in some other way or at some later date.

A helpful aid to use or at least to have available is a simple but fully explanatory guide which this should explain what the LOI is, where it meets, when it meets and at the time at which its meetings commence.

The guide should contain a simple but clear explanation of why the LOI exists, what it seeks to achieve, the new member's involvement within it and should explain that, although the Lodge meeting itself is the outward sign of the proficiency of the members, the LOI is where the heart resides and where the growing takes place.

It should be explained that the LOI is not the place where brethren come to learn words parrot-fashion but a place where, since it meets far more regularly than the lodge itself, the brethren can get to know each other in the relaxed atmosphere which is noticeably different from that which prevails at the lodge meetings.

The following suggested type of letter may assist Brother Preceptor in forming his own guide as related to his particular Lodge of Instruction.

It is not suggested that this is the finite letter to use but it is a starting point and covers the majority of the points which Brother Preceptor would wish to impart to the latest addition to the lodge.

Dear Brother

THE LODGE OF INSTRUCTION

You will undoubtedly have heard from your proposer the phrase 'Lodge of Instruction' and apart from a brief explanation of its place in the overall masonic system, being 'the place we go to learn the ritual', you will probably know little more about the reason it exists or what it hopes those who attend its meetings will achieve. This leaflet has been produced especially for newly-initiated brethren like yourself so that they can receive a fuller explanation of the reason for its existence.

As the name suggests this regular meeting of the members of the lodge takes place at .... on .... of each week from the first .... in September through to the last week in May of each year commencing at .... pm.

The LOI exists under the auspices of the lodge itself which is responsible for its correct operation. The lodge member responsible for its operation is known as the Preceptor which is another way of saying teacher. The atmosphere within the LOI is far less formal than that which you experienced at your initiation.

Dress is less formal than at the lodge meetings although due decorum is requested.

When you have completed your third degree you will be able to obtain a book of the ritual used by this lodge and from reading that book you will be able to ascertain just what has to be absorbed during the years which lead up to you becoming the Master of the lodge.

You may consider that to mention such matters which are unlikely to occur for many many years at this early stage in your membership is surprising. This is done quite deliberately to demonstrate to you that your training for the highest office in the lodge commences very soon after your initiation. You will be reassured to know that you will not be required to progress at a speed greater than that which you personally so desire.

The LOI has an overall plan which covers the full season of masonic activity usually covering a period of nine months and this is produced and handed to members at the start of every season. New members such as yourself will be gradually introduced into the system, carrying out roles within the LOI which are not demanding but which will enable you to start understanding the shape and content of each degree.

Do not be frightened of or reject out of hand the book of masonic ritual used by your lodge as an impossibility for you to read and retain for it is surprising just how soon it can and is absorbed by a regular weekly attendance at the LOI.

There are a few ground rules which should be understood from the outset and these are simple to remember. The Preceptor is in complete charge and his word should NEVER be challenged during a Lodge of Instruction meeting. The only person who should give instruction audibly is the Preceptor and the brethren attending the LOI, no matter how skilled in ritual they might be, should NEVER interrupt the proceedings with their own observations. A plan for learning exists and a copy will be given to you upon receipt of your request.

Never be afraid to ask questions of the Preceptor for that is the reason he is there, to train, inform, explain and generally enthuse those with less knowledge of masonic matters than himself. If it should be that you ask a question to which he does not have an immediate answer, he will undoubtedly return to the subject at a future meeting.

There are many good books which can be bought to advance your knowledge and an approved list can be obtained from QCCC Sales Ltd at Freemasons' Hall, Great Queen Street, London, WC2B 5BA. Telephone No 071 405 7340. Fax No 071 404 8131.

I look forward to greeting you at your first Lodge of Instruction meeting when it will be my pleasure to explain to you the details of our meetings and how you may obtain the maximum benefit from your attendances.

. . . .
Preceptor

Chapter 4:

That First Visit to the LOI

Our first view of virtually everything we experience in life usually gives us one of the following reactions, surprise, delight, shock, horror, disappointment, pleasure or amazement. It is therefore 'vital', I repeat the word 'vital', that the first visit to the LOI made by any brother is one which will fix the impression clearly in his mind of happiness in a relaxed atmosphere but most of all fun, for without fun what a miserable occasion the LOI would be to be sure.

Remember that first impressions count, and can take a very long time to dispel, especially if the first visit to the LOI is not handled with great care and prior thought.

Speaking now from ten years personal experience of handling a totally new Lodge of Instruction for a newly consecrated lodge in which the membership came from a variety of ritual backgrounds was indeed fun, for the vagaries of the various rituals ground into the minds of the brethren (who were now Founders) in their mother lodges was hard to change. However, it did have one very good effect which was to allow each member to sympathize with his fellow founders when it came to the different nuances of the new and so far totally different ritual (for many) which he was being asked to learn.

A very good and thoroughly recommended practice is for the Preceptor to ask the newly-made brother to sit beside him for the first two or three visits to the LOI and quietly explain to him the basic sections which the ritual sets out to encompass.

What then are these sections?

Firstly there is the entry of a candidate without knowledge, experience or ability. He is led everywhere blindfolded and instructed in what he should do and when he should do it, just as a new and inexperienced child might be so led and instructed. He has to take on trust all that is being said to him by his guide and those whom he meets whilst blindfolded.

Secondly he has imparted to him some instruction and he is then obligated whilst blindfolded after which his vision is restored and he is entrusted with signs and tokens. He is next asked questions on those things he has so far been shown and to which he is required to give answers, all of course with the ever present aid of brother Junior Deacon.

Thirdly he is finally rewarded by being given a badge of distinction with a full explanation of its significance and meaning.

Once the newest LOI member can grasp these three quite separate sections of the degree he can start to understand how the verbiage attached to each of them is constructed, and what that collage of words is meant to indicate.

NEVER, I repeat NEVER start your early instruction with words, begin with the story, the candidate who knows nothing comes to the door of the lodge where someone (the Tyler) has to answer on his behalf.

After that comes the entry into the lodge during which he is conducted around the room and introduced to the Junior and Senior Wardens whilst still unable to see, (the reason for this you will explain is in case he decides NOT to take the Obligation of an Entered Apprentice Freemason in which case he can leave the lodge room without let or hindrance for he has seen and heard nothing).

He is next asked to repeat an Obligation in which he signifies his agreement to keep the secrets of Freemasonry and he seals that Obligation in a time honoured manner. As a result he is entrusted with the signs and words of a Freemason.

He is then taken to the two most senior officers in the lodge after the Worshipful Master and presented as a freemason and is asked to give proof of his being a member. After this he is invested with the badge (apron) of his rank on the instructions of the Master of the lodge.

His poverty is tested, and the explanation for that is given to him by the Master (symbolism). The working tools of the degree are explained to him and moralized upon (symbolism).

He is allowed to retire to regain his composure and restore his exterior clothing (called personal comforts). He is readmitted to the lodge and is given a fuller explanation of what is expected of him in his duty to the Supreme Being; to his neighbour; and to himself; as a member of society and as a member of the fraternity.

This explanation is given to him by means of the delivery of the Ancient Charge. He is then seated next to the Senior Deacon who cares for him during the remainder of the meeting.

Such you will tell him in your short explanation of the first degree is the sequence of events that comprises virtually every degree in Freemasonry. They can be simplified by remembering that we are talking about Ignorance, Trust, Enlightenment, and Explanation and Reward. These four segments when learned and understood will go a long way towards easing the path of learning of our newly-made member.

Chapter 5:

The Annual Plan

Most if not all efficiently run organizations have an annual plan of operation in which is clearly stated what it is hoped to achieve during the year and when and how that which is planned is going to happen so that all who participate in it may be aware of the total achievement being striven for as well as the part of each participant in the overall plan.

Precisely the same care and planning needs to be accorded to the running of the Lodge of Instruction and this chapter of the book is written with this aspect very much in mind.

We shall assume for the purpose of this book that we are going to allocate a number to each brother in the lodge who is currently an officer and will include as well those who are Stewards. We shall give to the Senior Warden the designation Brother number 1, the Junior Warden Brother number 2, the Senior Deacon Brother number 3, the Junior Deacon Brother number 4, and the Inner Guard Brother number 5, with the remaining seven numbers from 6 to 12 being available for such other brethren as may be able to attend on given occasions.

If the Lodge of Instruction has a regular attendance of more than twelve members then it is suggested that the work of the various offices is divided up during the ceremony thereby giving everyone present an opportunity to participate.

The chart which follows will, if carefully observed, ensure that each officer participates only in the rehearsal of the offices which are senior to that which he actually holds, his current office being rehearsed on the LOI officers' nights.

The list covers a period of fourteen weeks with the fifteenth week starting the plan from the beginning once again. The lodge officers' nights can be fitted into the listing wherever necessary and the format can be continued after such officers' nights have been held. Assuming four lodge meetings a year, this would mean that two rehearsal nights could be held for the existing list of officers prior to each meeting, thereby making eight in total. It should in these circumstances be possible for the plan as shown to be operated twice in each year in addition to the eight officers' nights. Thus a lodge of instruction season would last 14 weeks plus 14 weeks plus 8 weeks, thirty-six weeks in all.

It has been found from personal experience that such a plan printed and issued prior to the start of the Lodge of Instruction season, showing the names of the brethren occupying the various offices throughout the season, assists considerably both the Preceptor as well as those who attend.

Brethren are made aware what is expected of them well in advance thus giving them the opportunity to rehearse the work they are scheduled to carry out and, if necessary, to study the ritual and learn that which is so far unlearned.

It also assists the Preceptor to know well in advance the names of those brethren who will be absent so that the offices thus now unfilled can be allocated to the younger members who may not have been allocated a role for that particular week.

This means of course a better overall control of the LOI with improved performance from those attending and the opportunity for the more enthusiastic younger members to 'fill in' for those who for whatever reason are unable to be present.

There are of course other benefits from following such a plan not least of which is that the incoming Master will have a first hand experience of those brethren whom he may well be asking to act as his officers during the ensuing year.

The Master can then judge their enthusiasm, dedication and aptitude for the office which he has in mind for them to occupy and decide whether or not their progress and performance in the Lodge of Instruction indicates their suitability for the proposed role in the lodge itself.

Another benefit is that the incoming Master will have the opportunity on a weekly basis of working with his potential officers thereby building a cohesive team who become used to working together. Further, their performance as a group can be assessed for

THE PLAN

Date	Degree	WM	SW	JW	SD	JD	IG	Members
WK 1	FIRST	A	B	C	D	E	F	A = BRO 1
WK 2	SECOND	B	C	D	E	F	G	B = BRO 2
WK 3	THIRD	C	D	E	F	G	H	C = BRO 3
WK 4	FIRST	D	E	F	G	H	I	D = BRO 4
WK 5	SECOND	E	F	G	H	J	K	E = BRO 5
WK 6	THIRD	F	G	H	J	K	L	F = BRO 6
WK 7	FIRST	G	H	J	K	L	M	G = BRO 7
WK 8	SECOND	A	B	C	D	E	F	H = BRO 8
WK 9	THIRD	B	C	D	E	F	G	J = BRO 9
WK 10	FIRST	C	D	E	F	G	H	K = BRO 10
WK 11	SECOND	D	E	F	G	H	J	L = BRO 11
WK 12	THIRD	E	F	G	H	J	K	M = BRO 12
WK 13	FIRST	F	G	H	J	K	L	
WK 14	SECOND	G	H	J	K	L	M	

its strengths and weaknesses thereby allowing corrective action to be taken if necessary within the confines of the Lodge of Instruction.

The annual plan can therefore be seen to have many 'spin off' benefits which may not be immediately apparent when its compilation is being discussed and prepared.

From week 15 onwards the listing is simply repeated thereby giving twenty-eight weeks of normal LOI instruction plus a further eight weeks of Lodge Officers' rehearsal nights, making in total a plan covering thirty-six weeks. If you therefore multiply each officer's place on the duty rota above by two you will see the opportunities each has to fulfil each office as listed.

As was stated at the start of this chapter, no efficient business would consider entering a new year of trading without a plan prepared well in advance covering 'what it hoped to achieve', 'how it was going to achieve it', 'who and how competent were the people responsible for ensuring the plan worked', and what was the fall-back situation should any of the parameters used prove to be faulty during operation. Precisely the same factors should apply to the Lodge of Instruction plan for the year.

A good Preceptor ALWAYS has a substitute in mind in the event that a lodge officer suddenly finds he cannot be present at a given meeting. Planning in advance for the unexpected is no different from taking out insurance on one's own home, is it? We always hope disaster will not occur but we are prepared in the event that it does.

Chapter 6:

The Enormity of the Task

If the question 'do you feel competent to take a wide range of men from differing backgrounds and teach them to work together in the enacting of an ancient form of drama-like ritual all from memory' were to be posed to the average freemason it is virtually certain that none other than a masochist would answer 'yes'. Yet we ask precisely that level of ability from every Preceptor.

For Preceptors are charged with the task of teaching, encouraging, enthusing and to some degree coercing the brethren placed under their care. Fortunately the brother who accepts the role is usually sufficiently experienced to know from his own period of service in the craft that the actuality is nowhere as difficult as the problem posed in the written word.

Teaching brethren whose educational background can be as widely drawn as a Professor of Medicine to a publican, from a Managing Director of a multi-national company with a quarter of a billion pounds turnover to an unskilled factory worker, can and indeed does have its moments of surprise and sympathetic drama. Yes, these things really did happen to the writer during his ten years as a Preceptor. Such experience proved that it was not necessarily the highly educated brother or the high flying industrialist who found the ritual easiest to learn or indeed who, once having learnt a masonic degree, necessarily performed it with meaning and feeling.

The lesson to be learned here is that there is no ideal masonic ritualist, brethren bring to their delivery and performance of masonic ritual a wide variety of talents, pace, timing, emphasis, projection, diction, and movement (body language). All have their part to play in the meaningful delivery of the ritual during a ceremony.

Many brethren can learn the words, many more can and do deliver them without any feeling whatsoever just as one might recite a train timetable, accurate but boring beyond belief.

Ergo, we quickly realize the enormity of the task we undertake when we accept the role of the Preceptor of the lodge.

The following thought has kept this Preceptor going when he has on occasions wondered if he was the only one who cared about the perfection of the delivery, the meaning of the words, the emphasis placed exactly where it should be placed and the timing and clarity of the more dramatic parts of our ancient ritual—it may help you in your 'hour of need'.

This Preceptor has always held one cardinal belief where the delivering of masonic ritual is concerned, and that can be stated quite simply; that there never has been a brother, nor is there ever likely to be a brother, who enters a lodge and participates in a ceremony intending from the outset to give the worst performance that it is in his power to give.

If this is true and this writer believes it is, then the obverse must also be true which is that brethren who accept offices, albeit sometimes rather reluctantly, do so with the intention of giving of their best—what more can any Preceptor ask? Think on these things.

Chapter 7:

Learning Little by Little

When faced with a ritual book containing the three degrees of craft masonry the less than confident brother can well make the emotive, and sometimes final decision, that his knowledge of his own ability tells him he will 'never' be able to assimilate all this verbiage and that he would be far better advised to admit this now and not waste the time of others who are clearly more competent than he is. These words actually came from a man who held a Doctorate of Philosophy and who, ten years later, was an exemplary Master of his lodge.

Faced with a page of anything of some ten or twelve lines and being asked whether he could manage to learn this in a month, virtually every brother would say either 'yes' or that he would certainly do his best. Indeed few, if any, would turn down that request without some consideration.

This simple but none the less easily demonstrated example goes a long way to showing the new Preceptor how to begin the task of building confidence and encouraging the aptitude of the brother who has but recently joined the Lodge of Instruction. If we examine virtually any ritual book we will find that a page does not usually exceed thirty or so lines and there is on most pages at least one break in the printed wording.

Giving a member a small paragraph to learn will usually start to build his confidence and before you move him on to the next paragraph you will find that he has of his own volition already started to read through if not indeed begun to learn that which follows.

Tell him to learn the first degree and he will almost certainly give one of the following answers: 'I do not have the time at the moment'; 'I do not have the ability to study so much ritual as I never was a good learner at school'; 'I never realized I would have to do all this when I joined the craft'; 'I will leave it until I have more time'; 'Perhaps when I have retired I will be able to consider it again'. There are many variations to this theme but the truth is simple, you have asked for too much at one 'bite'. A couple of sentences, yes certainly one paragraph, perhaps even a short page, but twenty pages of ritual most certainly not, because it is a daunting task to almost anyone and no one, particularly a new member, wishes to look foolish in front of his friends.

What have we learned from this chapter so far? Firstly, a little at a time. Secondly, that a brother with a first class education has the same natural reticence and doubt as his less educated brother. Thirdly, success builds success which builds more success. It is important that every brother has a small task to achieve by the time of the next Lodge of Instruction meeting, no matter how small that task may seem—even learning the correct pronunciation of words can be a beneficial task to set and is most essential.

Chapter 8:

Festive Board Training

This chapter has nothing to do with the learning of masonic ritual word-wise, but it does have a lot to do with the effective running of the lodge overall.

How often have we attended an Installation meeting carried out with considerable competence, with the incoming Master installing his officers with a high degree of proficiency but who, upon arriving at the Festive Board and finding himself confronted with the official toast list, looks at it as though it is written in Chinese, having not a clue as to the correct pronunciation of the names or the content of the list itself or for that matter who does what and when?

He has apparently not been given any instruction whatsoever on how he should propose the various toasts, which should be grouped together and which honorific titles should or should not be included.

How can a Master be allowed to arrive at the highest office in the lodge after possibly some ten to fifteen years of service and be so patently ill-equipped for the task which confronts him?

We have now arrived at the point of this chapter which is the training of the Master-elect in general but with special emphasis upon the Festive Board.

It is an excellent plan for every Master-elect to be taken through the Festive Board proceedings from start to finish commencing with the list of those with whom he wishes to take wine. Caution an over enthusiastic Master-elect from extending his list beyond four or five, for the object is to include everyone but not to interrupt what should be the major opportunity for the brethren to indulge in social intercourse.

The Master of a lodge has a duty to ensure that the after proceedings are conducted with dignity and due decorum and, in

20

particular, that once he gavels, silence is immediate. The over-frequent use of the gavel is to be discouraged for such has entirely the reverse effect to that for which the festive board is held, namely to allow the brethren to join together in conversation and mutual fellowship. Further he should be told to retain the gavel in his possession and not allow anyone else to use it. He is the only one who has the authority to call the brethren to order whether it be in lodge or at the Festive Board.

Ideally the taking of wine should be dealt with between the first and main courses of a meal and if the following list is adopted we are quite sure it will meet with approval by the brethren and minimize gavelling.

In time this will become known by the members as a short interlude in the Festive Board procedure and that once these 'takings of wine' are completed there will be no further interruption to the proceedings before the 'official toasts' are commenced after the coffee has been served.

1. The Master with everyone.
2. The Master with Grand Officers.
3. The Master with the Initiate (if appropriate).
4. The Master with the Visiting Brethren.
5. The Master with the Past Masters and Officers of the Lodge.
6. The Master with the Master-elect (Election night only).

The order in which these toasts are taken may vary according to local custom and practice. It may be the custom of the lodge to use number five on installation nights only.

Turning now to the Official Toast list it is essential that the Master-elect should be taken through it several times perhaps starting whilst he occupies the office of Senior Warden. No Master should ever be allowed to arrive at his first Festive Board untried and untrained in the use of the Toast list. Ensure that military and honorific titles are omitted, except where civil titles and honorifics are sanctioned by local custom and practice or are recommended by Grand Lodge or the Provincial or District Grand Lodge in which the lodge is situated.

The subject of 'masonic fire' if given in your lodge should be handled with great care and due decorum. The Master should be instructed that when giving masonic fire it is never speeded up to the point whereby there is competition to see who can finish first and the senior and perhaps older brethren are not only unable to participate but also become annoyed with the younger members for their apparent disrespect to the Sovereign, the Grand Master, the Craft and the Lodge.

The Master-elect should be reminded that it is his duty to unite and not divide the lodge. He has a heavy responsibility to ALL the members both young and old alike.

Correct teaching in the Lodge of Instruction repeatedly given throughout the year will ensure that from the most basic and indeed earliest training, the correct message is communicated at all levels.

The Master has a further duty to ensure that the Festive Board is conducted with a clear timetable in mind. The brethren have a right to expect that time is not wasted and that the proceedings will be conducted with the minimum of time-consuming activities so that those who have trains to catch or long journeys to make are not forced to leave before the proceedings are ended.

The ideal length of speeches, when given, is no longer than three to four minutes. Longer speeches will frequently result in brethren turning to their neighbours to talk and the courtesy and dignity of the occasion is lost.

On occasions of particular merit, the meeting may well be enhanced by the visit of a Provincial or District Grand Master, his Deputy or one of his Assistants. When this occurs the visiting officer will usually be accompanied by a Provincial or District Grand Director of Ceremonies who will take charge of the proceedings ceremonially speaking, and this will usually include a large part of the Festive Board.

Such Directors of Ceremonies will of course introduce the Official he has brought and it is appropriate for the Master of the Lodge to have a SHORT speech of welcome prepared for use on such an occasion, rather than to make the stark announcement that: 'We will now drink a toast to' without any speech of welcome being given. Further, it is essential that the Master should know the correct pronunciation of the official's name and the exact rank he holds. It assists considerably in the projection of the Lodge image for the visiting officer to see and appreciate the fact that the Master himself has taken the time and trouble to prepare his work for the Festive

Board with care and consideration for his guests, of both high and low rank alike.

Finally we trust that Brother Preceptor will appreciate the importance of such Festive Board training and ensure that it is included in his overall plan for the year of work. It cannot be stated too clearly or too often that to have an excellent ceremony performed within the lodge room but followed by an uncontrolled and ill-prepared Festive Board is a great disappointment to the members and their guests. Moreover it demonstrates most glaringly that the Master has put all his effort into learning the ritual, but for the remainder of his responsibilities at the lodge meeting he has received little if any training whatsoever and that Brother Preceptor is entirely 'down to you'.

Chapter 9:

A Step at a Time

Our newly-integrated brother has learned his small part in the proceedings and is now attending the Lodge of Instruction to show what he has been able to achieve. He quickly realizes that the part of the ritual he has learned has to interface with a plethora of other parts being delivered by perhaps equally unsure and hesitant recently-initiated members. He may be word perfect, he may be full of confidence, he may possibly place emphasis on the words where such is not called for, but whatever he does and however he does it, he needs to feel that his efforts have been appreciated and that he is a 'success' no matter how great or how small.

Such a feeling of 'having done well' will enthuse him to try to take another small part for the following week even though it is only of six or seven lines. He is being slowly taught by example that progress does come to those who try, and whilst the level of efficiency which he witnesses from Past Masters and those who are much nearer the Master's chair than he is at this time, is greater than his own, he has nevertheless made a start in the order of things and moreover he is making progress. A kindly word of appreciation from brother Preceptor at this stage in his masonic career will work wonders for it will give him the determination to take on another task even though it may only be a further six or seven lines of ritual.

Our newly-initiated brother is very similar to that small child in that everything he attempts is strange, untried and new, he has never seen or heard it before and he will metaphorically 'fall down' many times before he starts to gain a degree of perfection.

Whilst we watch the child with awe and wonder and encourage every little progress with words of encouragement and happiness we should also realize that, although much older, the same basic recognition of the efforts made and achievement gained is fundamental to every human being no matter who or what they happen to be, pauper or millionaire.

Moral—kind words work wonders.

Chapter 10:

Encouragement

Human nature is such that we all have a desire to feel needed and necessary and this applies no less to the members of the Lodge of Instruction than to one's own immediate circle of family and friends. Encouragement is the greatest single asset available for the Preceptor to award in liberal quantity, particularly where an unsure brother is or has been struggling with a particular piece of ritual which he simply cannot seem to master.

Encouragement takes many forms starting with the kind word at the conclusion of the Lodge of Instruction to the private word given or sent in a letter to a brother whose achievement has been particularly noteworthy at a lodge meeting. We can all differentiate between someone who has tried hard to learn the ritual as opposed to one who has but given scant thought to the responsibility of his office. To send a short note to the brother who has given his utmost effort will renew his determination to succeed and produce for you as the Preceptor a pupil whose dogged determination will thrive under your tutorship.

Confidence often shown in ample measure at a lodge meeting can in fact be a cover for a feeling of deep insecurity and a Preceptor who knows his pupil's ability and can tell when he is 'under pressure' will be able, with the help of an 'encouraging word', to make that pupil feel he has a friend who both knows and cares about his struggle with the ritual.

The feeling of isolation which can be felt by anyone 'performing' in front of his brethren for the first time even at the LOI is perhaps immeasurable by most of us for we are not all extroverts by any means and some find speaking in front of others very difficult.

Emotions range from embarrassment to sheer fright, from the feeling of potential failure to looking a fool in front of the senior members of the lodge, and thereby being judged as 'stupid'.

Such is the time for the Preceptor to start to build the brother's confidence by telling him how everyone in front of whom he will be carrying out his piece of ritual has experienced precisely the same sense of potential failure or fear that is plaguing him at this time and perhaps even more particularly that everyone, but everyone, will be aware how he is feeling whilst he carries out his part in the ceremony.

Such knowledge does go a long way towards helping a brother to come to terms with his feelings of inadequacy which may or may not be warranted. Many newly appointed officers simply cannot accept that the performance which they have just given within the lodge room or the LOI was satisfactory both to the lodge and to the Preceptor of the Lodge of Instruction. We all know from our own personal knowledge of the years we have spent in the craft that it is not what anyone says to you which counts, it is your own expectation of yourself which means most in your satisfaction or otherwise of the occasion.

Encouragement therefore can take many forms and ALWAYS remember that no brother ever comes to a meeting of the Lodge of Instruction or to one of the lodge itself intending to perform his part in the proceedings badly. Each brother does the best he can for this is the nature of man. Some by the very fact that they are human beings will perform better than others and it is not always the best educated or the brainiest whose performance is the most satisfying. Each deserves such encouragement as befits the occasion and believe me brother Preceptor encouragement genuinely given is the most acceptable award you can ever give to someone who really is giving of his best.

A kind word at an early stage can and will give you untold dividends in the years which lie ahead, to say nothing of making a friend for life.

Chapter 11:

The Benchmarks

Benchmarks are the achievements which you set a brother to accomplish in each stage of his development in the Lodge of Instruction, so that his progress through the offices of the lodge can be planned and measured.

This chapter is therefore one of setting goals and achievements for the 'average brother', in other words, someone who is neither exceptional in his learning ability nor who finds learning difficult if not almost impossible.

It will be the task of every Preceptor to ascertain in his own way just where the members of his Lodge of Instruction fit into the plan which is suggested as being ideal for the 'average' member.

Clearly where the more advanced brother is concerned he will quickly absorb the written word and progress at his own speed and ability possibly surprising everyone by his enthusiasm and dedication. Such brethren are the exception and whilst brother Preceptor will always be pleased to have as many as possible of this ability in his stable of learning, he will nevertheless realize all too quickly that the vast majority of those under his wing come under the banner of average. Such brethren have to dedicate themselves to a regular period of study if they are to reach a satisfactory level of achievement.

Assuming a seven-year programme of learning, the following suggested list is designed to take a brother through to the office of Master with the minimum of pressure and involves learning on the average far less than two lines of ritual each week.

Year 1. When a Steward he should learn the First degree.
Year 2. When still a Steward he should learn the Second degree and rehearse the First degree regularly.

Year 3. When the IG, learn the charge after Initiation and rehearse the First and Second degrees regularly.

Year 4. When the JD, learn the Third degree and rehearse the First and Second degrees regularly.

Year 5. When the SD, learn the Second Degree Tracing Board and continue to rehearse the First, Second and Third degrees regularly.

Year 6. When the JW, learn the Installation Ceremony and continue to rehearse the three degrees.

Year 7. When the SW, learn the Investiture of Officers and continue to rehearse the Installation Ceremony and the three degrees.

Year 8. When the WM, learn the Inner Working. Perform the ceremonies. Install his successor and have a very happy, successful and memorable year as Master of the Lodge.

As can be seen from the foregoing listing, if the learning process is taken stage by stage the newly-initiated candidate will have a steady, gradual progress through the three degrees of craft Freemasonry without fear of being chased by the Preceptor and being asked to perform outside his own learning 'curve'.

The listing as shown will allow for a gradual and progressive absorption of the ritual together with the discipline of looking at the ritual book every day. The ready acceptance by example based on past results will show just how easy it is to absorb what at first appeared to be an impossible amount of ritual.

If this plan for learning is adopted by the Preceptor and adequate records are maintained, then each Preceptor will know that a brother of three years' membership should be in the process of learning the items listed under Year 3.

This listing is designed to give the Preceptor ample warning of a brother who is falling behind in the learning process and gives time for him to arrange some private tuition if this is thought to be desirable. Alternatively perhaps a short private talk with the brother concerned will disclose what he believes can be arranged to enable him to 'catch up' in his learning curve.

Chapter 12:

Projection and Audibility

The Master of the lodge is effectively the Chairman of the meeting and whilst it is desirable that he is thoroughly competent in the delivery of the ritual during the ceremonies which he will perform during his year in office it is also equally desirable that he is seen to be in charge of the lodge in every sense of the word.

The word 'projection' has a number of definitions, one of which indicates something which stands out in front of all others. Such should be the effect of the Master of a lodge when he is exercising his rightful role during the meeting. Many competent brethren can handle the verbiage, many others can satisfactorily deliver the ritual, but the brother who can also project his personality into the delivery of all that he does will quickly become a focal point of attention as well.

Projection takes many forms from the use of pace, timing, delivery and body language together with good diction and essential clarity, each of which are dealt with in the following chapters. Projection therefore is the combined use of these many facets and will naturally differ from brother to brother.

Being in charge because you have been installed into the Master's chair is one thing, but by using the many 'attention compelling' facilities available to him the average Master can become an outstanding one.

Projection of one's personality can be seen at virtually any time on television and one only has to look at politicians, leaders of industry and newscasters to see the many forms such projection can be used to advantage.

The manner in which one would speak in a lodge or at a Festive Board would be quite different from that when one was holding a face to face conversation say in a car or over lunch. Putting on a 'projection overcoat' is no bad thing and can assist the shy, unsure, insecure brother at the time when he most needs to feel confident.

To talk approximately eighteen inches above the head of the Senior Warden helps, for this ensures that the Master is looking up and it reminds him to speak up, it also makes certain that his volume is adequate for he will quickly realize that to reach the Senior Warden he really does have to speak up.

It is no bad thing for the Master and his Senior Warden to have a private signal between them which will indicate to the former when his volume level has dropped to a point which is hardly audible to the latter and that he requires to increase his strength of audibility if he is to be heard clearly around the lodge room.

Perfecting such projection can bring great benefits to the brother in his life outside the lodge for it can build his confidence so that should the occasion arise for him to speak in public he is capable of doing so and can accept the challenge.

Freemasonry and the performance of its rituals can assist in many facets of one's private life.

Chapter 13:

Pace, Timing and Delivery

This heading might well appear to refer more to the athlete than to a book for Preceptor of Lodges of Instruction but the same requirements apply whether one is running a race or delivering a ceremony in a masonic lodge.

So much of the ritual we use comes to us from the verbiage of years past and it is true to say that much of it would benefit from re-writing and being put into correct English. Until such time as that major re-write takes place we are left with ritual books full of sentences and paragraphs most of which can be expressed in a variety of ways depending upon where the definition or emphasis of certain words is placed. This is where the use of pace, timing and delivery come into play.

Emphasis and feeling can be placed upon certain words which with an added pause before the next word or sentence is delivered will give that word strength and meaning.

An example of this can be illustrated if we take the words used by the candidate when answering the questions from the first to the second degree. In the reply to the Master's question "Who are fit and proper men to be made Freemasons" the answer is "Brotherly Love, Relief, and Truth". Without the benefit of a pause between the words Brotherly Love (pause) Relief (pause) and Truth, the meaning and impact of these impressive and meaningful words can be lost entirely.

How often have we heard the totally correct answers given to these questions but equally, given without feeling, pace or timing thus ruining the delivery?

This is but a very simple illustration of what is meant by Pace and Timing. Ordinary words can be given feeling and definition by the use of Pace and Timing and these assets are to be encouraged when brethren are being taught how to deliver the ritual as well as in general communication within the lodge. Such tuition can well assist the newly-made brother in his private life as well, especially if in his business life he has to address audiences albeit perhaps no more than a dozen or so people at a time. To be able to deliver the spoken word with feeling, pace and good timing is an art-form to be learned and once learned never forgotten.

Students who have decided that an acting profession is where their future lies are often given large passages of Shakespeare to learn and recite simply so that their delivery, pace, timing and diction can be assessed.

Whenever 'Hamlet' is produced on the London stage the principal actor is said to be either a first class, an indifferent, or a poor Hamlet. How can this be, for the words are the same every time they are uttered? The answer is that it is the way in which they are delivered that makes all the difference.

The message from this chapter is simple: 'It's not what you say, it's the way that you say it'.

Chapter 14:

Speech

In the previous chapter we dealt with Pace, Timing and Delivery. We now come to the thorny question of speech.

In its earliest days the British Broadcasting Corporation had a standard form of English which was to be used by all who were engaged by that broadcasting giant. Those who wished to be employed by this new monolith in communication were required to conform to the standards laid down for the spoken word. A pronunciation department was created and still exists to this very day. All news scripts are subjected to intense scrutiny for strange foreign words, particularly place names, names of foreign diplomats and dignitaries, heads of governments, proper names of products and the like.

Such is the desire of the BBC to attain perfection in the delivered word that this whole department is on duty twenty-four hours a day, seven days a week, the sole purpose of which is to ensure that any word which might have different or alternative ways of being pronounced is in fact delivered in the way the BBC desires and woe betide any announcer who delivers it in other than the approved manner.

Sadly such is not the case in Freemasonry, for in our masonic ritual we have many, many words which we allow those whom we teach to pronounce in any way they feel is appropriate.

The Preceptor of the Lodge of Instruction has a duty to teach good pronunciation because once the new member pronounces any word wrongly and is allowed to go uncorrected he will for the future continue to use that pronunciation probably for the rest of his days. Check him at the first hurdle and he will remember your advice and use the approved method knowing that this is the right way to pronounce the difficult word which he has possibly never heard before.

There are many such words in our rituals and here I would quote a few of them in the first degree: 'competency', 'piety', 'delineate', 'animosity', 'amicably', 'characterize', 'approbation', 'opulence', 'derogatory', 'inviolable', 'extort', 'acquiescence'.

Clearly other examples can be found in every degree in the ritual and it is not suggested that any brother will find the foregoing examples either difficult or impossible to pronounce. What is suggested, however, is that some brethren may have their own pronunciations used over many years which whilst perfectly satisfactory within their family unit simply are not acceptable when addressing the lodge during a masonic ceremony. Incidentally, common errors in the Royal Arch are 'Hag-ee-eye' instead of 'Hag-eye' and 'Sign-ee-eye' instead of 'Sign-eye'.

Care is needed when a correction is suggested to a brother, for here we are close to the fine line where possible embarrassment might be caused, and it is the skilled Preceptor who can handle such occasions with due decorum by explaining that 'in Freemasonry' we pronounce that word in 'this' way.

The use of the phrase 'in Freemasonry' does away with the suggestion that he has been pronouncing the word incorrectly for many years, it simply means that 'Freemasonry' has a different way in which to say or use that particular word. Tact and diplomacy can work wonders in such a situation.

Local accents or brogues always add a special something to the pronunciation of words and it is to be hoped that we shall never reach the stage where we have to change the way in which brethren from our shires speak, so that they conform to the standard BBC method.

The English language correctly spoken with good diction, delivered in a confident warm and feeling manner, is a delightful means of communication and when combined with masonic ritual delivered with correct pronunciation and good timing makes for pleasure unimagined.

Chapter 15:

Body Language

How often we listen to the words of the speaker telling us what appears at first hearing to be a factual statement about a series of events or happenings and yet something is not right. Something reduces what is being said by a meaningful percentage, detracting from the story, causing it to be less believable than might otherwise be the case.

If we examine what has been said and then the 'way' in which it has been said we quickly realize that the person delivering the discourse has been communicating negative body language.

What then is negative body language? It can be as simple as the posture of the person when speaking, to a disinterested expression on the face, to a constant and perhaps annoying action such as looking at a watch or looking at the ceiling or letting the concentration factor lapse from the audience to whom the speaker should be delivering the talk with emphasis and feeling.

Therefore it is important not only to have a command of the ritual with an accuracy which is acceptable but with the combined assets of timing, diction, pace, emphasis and feeling together with good confident body language. A brother of moderate ability can perform at a level well above a more ritually capable brother who does not have such assets which are essential for a meaningful delivery.

We all use body language whether we realize it or not, the way we stand, the way we sit, relaxed or tense, smiling or severe, every posture communicates a message and unless we are careful we can communicate exactly the opposite message to that which we intend.

A skilled actor communicates with all his senses, his posture, his timing, his variation of pitch and tone, his facial expressions, his hands, his demeanour and last his voice.

We have all heard the expression 'selling a story' and a person who can do so invariably uses most if not all of the senses outlined in the previous paragraph and this ability marks out the successful and outstanding from the moderate and mediocre.

Turning now to our masonic ritual we will all have heard the perfectionist who has learned the words and repeats them without fault and yet somehow there is no feeling, no sense of communication, no sincerity, just words, words, words, delivered exactly as they are printed, flat and without feeling.

How much more we tend to appreciate a brother whose ability to deliver ritual with such perfection is seriously in deficit but who can give the ceremony he is performing such feeling, timing, diction and pace, whose volume and definition brings to life the words he is speaking albeit that he requires the occasional prompt.

Perhaps more importantly we should always remember that oft quoted but nevertheless true statement that ceremonies are performed for the benefit of candidates who have never heard the ritual before and who are for the most part left with the ambiance of the occasion as their most poignant remembrance of the ceremony.

The memory of the drama in the ceremony, the movements around the lodge room, some of the signs and words, will be just about all our newly-made brother will remember. If the ceremony is well delivered with good timing, posture, pace and feeling combined with good body language, the candidate will be impressed far more than might be the case with a perfectly delivered ceremony word-wise without any of these other attributes.

Body language therefore is a major factor when performing any ceremony and is equally important when any officer performs his duty such as a Director of Ceremonies, Deacon or Inner Guard, for with effective body language each in their own way can considerably add to their own performance if care and thought is given to this aspect of their role within the lodge.

Good posture when sitting, standing or speaking is essential for each officer is playing a part, each has a duty to play that part to the best of his ability for the benefit of the 'team' and of course for those who are there to 'observe and be silent'.

You may find the following unbelievable but you can prove it for yourself by trying it. If when using the telephone you smile when you are speaking, you will transmit that smile through the telephone to the person listening at the other end. Why not use the same technique when speaking to your audience? It makes you so much more believable.

Chapter 16:

Diction and Clarity

We have already referred to the words in the heading of this chapter several times in the preceding chapters of this book but they are so vitally important that they deserve a chapter entirely to themselves.

Diction is the ability to choose the correct words to fit the occasion and the word 'diction' itself comes from the same family as does the word dictionary. For the most part, in the rendering of masonic ritual we seldom have to utilize the facility we each have to use our diction to maximum advantage, for the compilers of the ritual in their original forms and latterly the ritual associations which control the more modern editions, have carried out that task for us.

We do, however, have ample opportunity to use good diction when we address the lodge during occasions other than ritual ceremonies and also of course when asked to speak at the Festive Board.

Training in the selection and use of good diction will very probably have been a feature of our basic education and of correct English, for it is that which will have been built up over many years. The ability to select precisely the right word from the thousands we each have in our memory banks is an art form, but one which can be improved with training as well as by accepting as many opportunities to exercise that ability as present themselves.

The author well remembers a simple but effective means of improving both shyness and speaking ability which he experienced in his teenage years. The teacher taking this particular class placed ten or so subjects on slips of paper and placed them in a receptacle. Each person was instructed to take one slip from those offered and immediately stand and speak for one minute on the subject mentioned.

The teacher pressed a timer set for one minute as well as a tape recorder so that what was said could be discussed and the choice of words considered by the assembled students so as to discover in a group setting whether a better selection of words could have been used. This may seem to be a basic if not simplistic way of building confidence and assisting those who wish to improve and increase their public speaking ability but it does work, of this you may be assured. Those who have participated in this type of training will, we are sure, vouch for the benefits they obtained.

There was a three-fold benefit to be obtained from such an exercise. Firstly it allowed those participating to gain confidence by speaking in front of others. Secondly it allowed the speaker to choose his own words and combine them with his or her own knowledge of the subject stated. Thirdly it allowed both the teacher and the student to examine the choice of words and to a degree analyse which were good words and suitable for the subject in hand.

It also taught the rest of the assembled students the manner in which they could best deal with a sudden appeal to speak without prior warning.

This is an admirable way to train, build confidence and improve diction all at the same time. If you, brother Preceptor, have a number of somewhat shy, retiring and perhaps even tongue-tied brethren you might find that such an evening or two would help to give 'your charges' the confidence which they lack at this time. You do not have to hold such an evening at the LOI, it can be done quite privately on a specially organized evening set aside for this 'special confidence boosting training'. Try it, you might be surprised.

Clarity simply refers to clearness. When applied to the spoken word it means the correct use of the vowel sounds and the ability to use the mouth and lips to advantage so that the words which are uttered are delivered in a meaningful manner. Thereby the content of the words so expressed will communicate in totality the meaning, sense and implication of the statement made so that the recipients thereof have a full and complete understanding of what is being uttered.

Good diction when combined with clarity can turn an unsure and moderate speaker into a confident public speaker to whom his fellow brethren as well as the visitors are always delighted to listen no matter how often or on which subject he is called upon to address them.

The lesson to be learned here is that with training even the most unsure persons can be raised to a level of confidence in a few short months which will do much for them as human beings as well as producing able public speakers. They are also much more fun to listen to as well.

For private practice away from the rest of his brethren it can benefit the individual considerably if he reads a chapter of a book and records what he says on a cassette. He can then play it back to ascertain the message he is communicating. It really is surprising just how often a brother has never heard his own voice and has no idea at all how he sounds to those who have the task of listening to him. The one thing this author will promise the reader is that this exercise will most decidedly ensure a greater care on the part of the speaker when he next 'stands and delivers'.

Chapter 17:

Good Days and Bad Days

The title of this chapter almost says it all, does it not?

There can be few of us who have not experienced both a day when we are on top of the world, everything is going right and the sun shines on us from sunrise till sunset. Equally we have all suffered those days when nothing, but nothing, appears to go right from the moment we wake in the morning until we place our weary body into bed in the late evening. On these latter days we sometimes wonder, do we not, why we ever got out of bed in the first place?

Brother Preceptor would be unwise if he did not keep very much in mind the fact that such 'good days' as well as 'bad days' will permeate the lives and happenings of his many and various charges.

One can hardly imagine that the brother who so successfully carried out the duties task of Senior Deacon in the third degree last week to the acclaim of both you as the Preceptor as well as his fellow brethren, is now the same brother who mumbles, fumbles and generally forgets his words and appears so incapable of carrying out the task which he was scheduled to perform this evening that you can scarcely believe he is the same man. Why should this be?

To answer this question we can but repeat some advice once given, many years ago, to the writer by a skilled and knowledgeable training officer who was first and foremost a psychologist who possessed considerable in-depth experience of human nature as it is particularly related to human behaviour patterns.

Most if not all good sound logical advice has a simple root and it was to this simple root that the writer's attention was directed. Each person (customer) who is visited by you during your normal working day as a representative of the company (said that training officer) will almost certainly have undergone many different personal and business experiences since you last called to see him some four to six weeks or so ago.

He may, said the training officer, have suffered a bereavement in his or his wife's family, one of his children may not be well, he may have some new unexpected financial problem which has arisen since you last saw him.

His business may have suffered a downturn, he may not be well or he may have received some worrying news related to his health, his bank manager may be putting financial pressures on him with which he cannot cope, or there may be a thousand and one other factors which could be the root cause for him to be a very different person from the one to whom you bid goodbye when last you met those few short weeks ago.

If you assume that this 'customer' is identical in every respect to the man whom you left recently it will show a great many weaknesses in your approach to say nothing of your misunderstanding of human nature and experience.

Firstly you have not shown him the most basic of common courtesies in ascertaining by the use of a few simple questions the reasons for his happiness or unhappiness and generally his current state of mind and present attitudes to his personal situation and to life generally.

Secondly you have missed an opportunity to get on his side of the counter 'metaphorically speaking' so that you can view such problems with him in a genuinely helpful and friendly manner. In so doing you will show him the warmth and caring side of your nature and thereby strengthen your personal relationship.

Thirdly you should know by reference to your own life that you are not the same unchanged person who last called on this customer, for you also have undergone many personal experiences both happy and otherwise since last you met him, so why assume that your customer has not?

What does the moral of this story tell us? Simply that if we substitute 'customer' for 'member of the LOI' we shall treat every one of our members with that same courtesy and consideration that we would show to a business customer, for the factors which we have examined are identical.

Every meeting of the Lodge of Instruction should be treated as a totally separate entity and without connection with the meeting which occurred the week before, except in the most cursory manner.

Many physical, mental or emotional occurrences could and possibly have played their part in the lives of our members since the last occasion we met and it would be an unwise Preceptor indeed who did not at the very least make some allowance for such a happening affecting the behaviour and performance of an otherwise diligent, capable member of the Lodge of Instruction.

The message then is very clear. A good Preceptor is a mixture of many parts; teacher, instructor, reference point, psychologist, guide, mentor, but above all a friend. Friends care about each other, so should a good Preceptor care about his members.

Chapter 18:

Building on Success

Success in any sphere brings with it a range of emotions which can have a variety of effects upon the recipient. Happiness is probably the most obvious, satisfaction with a good result after considerable hard work is another and the desire to press on and achieve even more success can and frequently is a driving force for the ambitious candidate.

Of those who attend university and achieve their bachelor degrees a number continue through to their masters' degree and some, the very few, press on for the attainment of their doctorate. Study can and should be fun but it can also be, for some, boring, frustrating, totally unsatisfying and unsettling. Why should this be so? Why should some find study satisfying and others carrying out exactly the same task find exactly the opposite?

The answer to two such questions is surely that since every individual is a unique construction of emotions, fears, driving forces, hopes and desires, to say nothing of his individual inherited genes, it is quite natural that such a person will react to a given situation in an entirely different way to his neighbour.

In chapter seven we dealt with the process of learning 'little by little' and this process does of course have considerable advantages.

But what of the bright new member who clearly demonstrates from his earliest of days in the LOI that here we have a person of exceptional ability and enthusiasm?

To him the learning of the ritual is as easy as reading the daily newspapers and his retention powers are demonstrably well above average. Brother Preceptor, you have a tiger by the tail and tigers are notoriously unpredictable, and 'yes' this author has met one or two in his years of teaching ritual.

With such a person you have a double problem, which if not identified and then handled correctly can terminate with you losing a member of considerable potential.

Firstly the driving factor which permeates everything such a brother undertakes will quickly indicate to him that he has a given time-frame in which to learn the ritual. It is almost certain that such a candidate will indeed achieve the levels of perfection he strives to attain for he is used to setting and achieving his own targets in life and knows from past experience what he can and perhaps equally as important what he cannot achieve. But what then, for here we have a bright attentive demonstrably capable individual who most decidedly will not be satisfied with merely attending and will in all probability quickly become bored because he likes challenges and will then start to look for pastures new to conquer.

It is highly possible if not probable that such a brother will move on to other degrees, other ceremonies and perhaps other interests entirely.

Secondly we have to recognize that we have to maintain his interest and harness his considerable learning abilities thus making him feel needed, wanted and necessary to the overall pattern of progress which every LOI will surely have as a target for its members.

Clearly here we have a candidate for individual instruction. A 'one off' member who will never be happy to learn at the pace of the class but one who will need our skilled attention to his needs if we are to retain and maximize the use of both a useful lodge officer as well as a future Past Master with many years to serve the lodge. One of the most difficult things to achieve with such a brother is to make him feel part of a team for he has almost certainly never achieved this feeling in anything he has ever done before. His scholastic achievements were very probably well above average and his teachers no doubt recognized him as well above the 'norm' and treated him as such. For him, working within the team unit will be strange as indeed will the requirement to rely on another member of the team to work in concert with him. He simply is not skilled in participating in co-operative or cohesive efforts.

Strangely enough working within a team may well be something he has wanted to do for most of his life but has never been allowed to do because of his individually recognized higher skills of learning.

How then do we deal with such a brother whose ability is well above average and whose powers of retention are exceptional?

If we have correctly ascertained the situation then we need to have a plan of action for such a potentially outstanding candidate which will differ from that which was set for our average members. The Charge after Initiation is a first and worthy starting point. The first and second degree tracing boards are another. The three addresses used in the Installation ceremony are a third. Such a brother would benefit from being exalted in the Royal Arch within three months after being raised to the third degree, for here he will see further challenges for his learning abilities, challenges moreover that will take him some time to achieve.

We are by this method taking a totally opposite course from that which we use with the insecure, diffident brother of little if any confidence who needs to be congratulated upon almost every line of the ritual he learns.

Some people like to take short walks, some take walking holidays, some climb mountains and some, the very few, climb Everest.

It's all a matter of degree, and so is learning. Each candidate needs challenges which can vary from the pronunciation of a difficult word to the absorption of a ceremony. By knowing the strengths and weaknesses of your charges and setting them their targets accordingly, you will indeed succeed beyond your wildest dreams.

Chapter 19:

Doves Fly Forwards

Few things in life if taught correctly in the first place will ever be forgotten and this applies as well to physical actions as well as to the spoken word.

Brother Preceptor should endeavour to give a small but meaningful demonstration of some part of the floorwork at every meeting of the LOI. What should he do? Let us examine a few of the important pieces of floorwork which can enhance or detract from the ceremonies we perform.

First and foremost, wands. Wands are badges of office and should be carried by the brother performing that office in a dignified manner. What is that dignified manner? A wand should be held in front of the body away from the right-hand side about the length from his elbow to his fingertips which on most people is between fifteen to eighteen inches. It should be held upright and not carried on the shoulder like an 'ancient pikeman' in the Lord Mayor's show.

Where two officers are to combine a dual role such as the Deacons, then a rehearsal between them to ascertain the height at which each will carry his wand will add to the overall dignity of the ceremony. Brethren of course vary in height and it is often the case that this can be as much as a twelve-inch differential in height between them. It is therefore essential that a rehearsal takes place to enable a satisfactory solution to be found.

Brother Deacons should be told from their first rehearsal in the Lodge of Instruction that 'Doves Fly Forwards', this is a lesson they will never forget for surely there can be few things worse than a badge of office being carried backwards and we are sure that the reader has seen plenty of those in his years in the craft.

Brother Director of Ceremonies and his assistant both have similar responsibilities and the placing of the wand in its holder after

48

the officer has sat down is, we suggest, the best way of accommodating this action rather than standing with his back to the Master fiddling with a wand-stand. It also allows for the ceremony to be continued by the Master without further delay. The Deacons should be so instructed at the LOI, after which they will automatically carry out this task without further reminders being necessary, for the action will become automatic. When standing to perform some part of the ceremony the wand should be released from its holder at the same time as the officer rises.

Wand-stands are not always placed where they should be and frequently this writer has seen the Senior Deacon's wand-stand placed on his left rather than his right which is its correct position. Tell your deacons designate at the LOI that they should ensure that 'their' wand-stand is always situated on the right before the start of the meeting and they will check at every meeting to make sure that this is so.

It is always a good practice to arrange for ALL officers to be present at least fifteen minutes before the stated commencing time of the meeting, this allows for replacements to be found should such prove to be necessary.

Demonstrate to your charges the correct way to hold a wand and how to move around the lodge whilst carrying it. Show them how to salute whilst carrying the wand and generally get them used to handling a wand in all the situations which will arise during a ceremony. When saluting in the first or third degrees, the wand should be transferred to the left hand. There is an exception when saluting in the second degree whilst standing in a stationary position as the wand should then be placed against the right shoulder. Once comfortable they will never again have the need to worry about this aspect of their office.

The Master and the Wardens when placed in their seats should give the Director of Ceremonies, so conducting them, a court bow (head only). This is not only the correct way of concluding a part of the ceremony, it also adds to the dignity of the occasion. The same court bow should be used when conducting anyone to the East to be invested with the collar of his office by the Master during an installation ceremony. You should also explain to your members that this court bow ought also be used when placing a Past Master into the Master's chair to perform a ceremony.

Train your charges to stand correctly, to keep their heads up when speaking, to ensure that the Deacons have correctly placed their left arm UNDERNEATH (rather than on top of) the candidate's when conducting him around the lodge, for this will give a greater pivotal control (try it and see).

The newly-appointed Chaplain will also frequently require instruction in the timing he uses in his role, as will the Immediate Past Master when he leaves his seat to adjust the Sq. and C's. All these actions if properly carried out add dignity to the whole meeting and it is after all just as easy to carry them out properly as it is to carry them out in a slovenly manner.

The turning of the Tracing Boards is another feature which should be covered at the Lodge of Instruction. A simple but effective system to be used is explained hereunder but its use will depend upon the weight and size of the Tracing Boards being used.

Let us assume for the purposes of this explanation that all three boards are facing the Junior Warden's pedestal.

For opening in the first degree simply turn one board. For opening in the second degree turn two boards. For opening in the third degree turn three boards.

For resuming in the second degree turn three boards. For resuming in the first degree turn two boards. For closing turn one board.

This method is simple to remember if taught properly from the beginning. Tell your students that the turning of the tracing boards is simple if they remember that on opening they are going up and on closing they are coming down.

Once we have opened in the first degree we open the board to show where we are. We then progress to opening in the second degree and therefore we take two boards and turn them. Progressing on once more to the third degree we take three boards and turn them. Simple but effective because we have related the first, second and third degrees with one, two and three boards. Coming back down we should think once more of where we are going. From three down to two means we handle three boards, from two down to one means we handle two boards and finally we close the lodge and the last board is turned.

Such handling of the tracing boards once rehearsed and perfected will become as natural as any other action taken in a lodge. It is both efficient in action and appears to the onlooker smooth in operation. In most cases it can be achieved with the use of one hand.

Try it in your Lodge of Instruction, you might find you like it, and then adopt it for use in your lodge.

Finally, let us consider when wands should be carried. When a Master appoints and invests his Deacons he says: "It is also part of your duty to attend upon Candidates . . . I therefore entrust you with this wand . . .". In other words, it is a ceremonial wand to be used in ceremonies but not in routine lodge business. It looks most undignified if a Deacon carries his wand in his right hand, as suggested in this chapter, and tries to balance a ballot box or minute book in his left hand, or if he carries it when changing the tracing boards.

Chapter 20:

Holding a Hand whilst Progressing

In a previous chapter we dealt with strength, now let us turn and deal with weakness.

We have all met those willing, dedicated brethren whose learning ability and desire to succeed is not matched by their ability to retain words, any words, even the words which they repeated so many times last week but now cannot remember even how the phrase begins. Strangely enough such brethren try so hard to achieve a degree of competence and yet despite all the effort only the sketchiest outline remains and they require a prompt at almost every other word. Someone once referred to such a situation as equivalent to drawing teeth without anaesthetic, painful in the extreme! Yet such brethren will come our way during our time in charge of the LOI.

What then can be done to help such a brother to his first benchmark of success? The answer surprisingly is a considerable amount of success for him does not have to be associated with the perfect delivery of a whole ceremony. The answer to this situation is a little at a time, even as little as getting him to close the VSL and say the words "Nothing now remains etc., etc., etc.," just twenty-four short words but words nevertheless to send him home feeling a real sense of achievement from that particular Lodge of Instruction.

All sound long-lasting structures have strong well laid foundations and building on such a firm base is the surest way of ensuring that we create an edifice of lasting ability for the future. To build such a secure base with a brother of modest ability needs to be achieved by what can only be described as a phrase at a time. What we are seeking to achieve here is not, surprisingly enough, the learning of words but the building of confidence in the brother carrying out the learning process, for there is truly nothing like success in any sphere to build even more success. The words really do not matter but his confidence in himself means more than can be imagined.

This may sound a rather trite remark to make but the truth is that it could well be the first time in the experience of the brother to whom we are referring that he has had any visible success in anything he has ever attempted.

We all strive and for the most part need success in our lives, be it for some the simple task of growing first class tomatoes, for others of achieving academic prowess, and yet for a third group of attaining physical success in athletics. The individual who has an ability in one may not necessarily have a similar ability in another, in fact it is almost certain he will not.

Therefore we all have differing abilities when related to any situation, but we also have one thing in common as well, and that is that if given sufficient training and encouragement we can ALL improve what we strive to do, and encouragement helps.

A good instructor will never set his sights too high when dealing with a brother of the type we are envisaging in this chapter, for it is as easy to destroy his confidence as it is to build him into a competent lodge officer.

Correctly handled he can be shown that his ability will eventually surprise even him and when his time arrives to be installed as Master of the lodge he will have the happiest of years because with your help and guidance he has achieved what at first appeared impossible. The man will grow in stature as well.

Such a brother needs his confidence lifting every time he tackles a new part of the ritual under your guidance. Ensure that you are controlling his learning and never let him jump ahead, control what he studies and ensure you test him on that task which you set him on the last occasion. He will enjoy showing you what he has achieved and you in turn should show him how pleased you are with his progress.

It really is quite amazing how such 'face to face' projects can work. A paragraph well learned and delivered with correct pronunciation in a confident manner at the correct level of audibility will build slowly and surely week by week an unsure, fumbling, incoherent member of the craft into a confident valuable officer of the lodge.

Private tuition is dealt with under Chapter twenty-three and ideally should be read in conjunction with this chapter.

Remember that satisfaction is in the eye of the beholder and as has been emphasized several times already in this book it is not what has been said to the brother as much as how he views his own performance or progress. That will count most with him—but, and it is a big BUT, by your actions and words you can 'confirm' his opinion that he is progressing.

We repeat for the record 'NEVER SET SUCH A BROTHER MORE THAN A FEW LINES TO LEARN AT A TIME'. If you do, you will fail in your intention to build confidence and simply confirm to him his opinion that this ritual really is beyond him.

Ignore these words of advice at your peril.

Chapter 21:

The Speed of the Convoy

This chapter is designed primarily for the newly-appointed Preceptor who has been given the responsibility of educating, moulding and cohesively pulling together the various talents of the members of a newly-consecrated lodge. The attendant problems associated when brethren from five or six different ritual backgrounds, each with its own variations, come together to form a new lodge can be and frequently are a real headache for the first Preceptor of this new lodge.

We have all been present at lodge meetings where the ritual is stated to be Emulation, Taylors, Logic or Universal or some other well known variant of those rituals, many of which have their roots as far back as 1813 and in some cases beyond, and yet the similarity to the version we use in our own lodge is purely coincidental and rather like a suit of clothes bought 'off the peg' which 'fits where it touches'.

This then is the dilemma of the newly-appointed Preceptor. How does he begin to tackle the problem of bringing together and creating a cohesive team of officers from such a variety of backgrounds who can and will work together for the benefit of the potential new lodge.

When such a group of brethren come together and gain permission for the formation of a new lodge they will be known collectively as 'Petitioners', for they do not become Founders until the day of the Consecration.

Brother Preceptor clearly cannot wait until after the 'big day' to start the process of drawing together the myriad of abilities already mentioned.

He should ascertain at the very first meeting of the brethren assembled to discuss the potential new lodge being formed precisely which ritual it is intended to use. It may well be that a ritual with which he is not familiar is to be suggested, in which case he will have to decide whether or not he can accept the task of training the prospective members, together with those who will become participants in the first formative and crucial years of operation.

The second important question which must be decided at this meeting is whether the brethren taking the Master's chair for (say) the first five years should all use their existing rituals or agree to conform to and use the mutually accepted 'new' ritual of the proposed lodge from its first day of operation, namely the Consecration.

Assuming the latter case to be the majority view, this might well mean that a number of the brethren previously expecting to progress through to the chair will change their minds. In that event a re-structuring may become necessary to achieve the desired first full five years of planning for the management of the lodge through its most important formative years.

If for example the ritual is now agreed and the first Master and Wardens are already using the agreed ritual, then clearly we have a situation where we know that for the first three years we have time to train, correct, build and enthuse those members who have the very difficult task of learning a new and so far totally strange ritual, a process which is infinitely more difficult to achieve than learning an original ritual.

Brother Preceptor now knows the size and scope of his challenge and can begin to make highly private and subjective judgements about the varying abilities of the brethren who will form his Lodge of Instruction. Prejudging any situation is unwise and we should be well advised to leave our new members a few meetings to settle into their totally new environment. Any draft of new recruits into the armed forces takes many weeks if not months of skilled instruction to turn them into a viable working unit. Such is also the case of brethren forming a new lodge who by working together and understanding the vagaries of another brother's performance of a ritual as he has been previously taught, begins the process of forming the unity so necessary in a cohesive team of any sort.

It must surely be appreciated by now that Brother Preceptor has been cast in the many varied roles of diplomat, teacher, and problem solver. Moreover he will have to use great tact and diplomacy if he is to succeed in his new task. An understanding gentle demeanour will assist him in his work.

To ask gently for the co-operation of a brother in carrying out a task in a certain way, when he has been carrying it out quite successfully for many years, in an entirely different manner will indeed require much patience on the part of the member, as well as the Preceptor. Each has to accept that there can only be one Preceptor in any Lodge of Instruction and that his direction should be obeyed without dissent.

One of the possible major difficulties which will be encountered will come from the rigid Past Master possibly wearing dark blue who refuses to change his ritual patterns of a lifetime and insists on doing things 'his way'.

Arguments must never take place at the Lodge of Instruction especially between senior officers. It is far better for such matters to be dealt with quite privately either after the LOI meeting or on some subsequent occasion. The method to be adopted is not one of confrontation but rather one of asking for the brother's help. Say quite clearly that you understand his point of view in wishing to do something a certain way and agree with him that you also carry out certain parts of the ritual in a different manner in your own lodge but, for the good of this new lodge, all must be prepared to give a little for the benefit of the new brethren who will follow and who in truth are those for whom the lodge was founded in the first place.

Asking for co-operation works, confrontation rarely does, and arguments regarding ritual are not what the role of a Preceptor is all about.

Brother Preceptor has been appointed to his role by the Founders and everyone should assist him in that role by accepting his word on all matters ritual-wise during a LOI meeting. If it should be that a member wishes to ask questions about something which to him is different or strange, then he should do so outside the LOI meeting, perhaps by calling the Preceptor on the telephone when they could have a completely private chat about the matter in question. This method ensures that there is no 'loss of face' on the part of either brother and that there is no public winner or loser of an argument— very important in a new lodge.

The title of this chapter is apposite to its contents, for the speed of the convoy (new lodge) will in all probability proceed at the speed of the slowest ship (least able officer). Much can be learned from the bringing together of brethren from differing ritual backgrounds to form and create what must surely be the greatest desire of all freemasons, namely the spreading of our order and the moulding of future members into worthwhile citizens who care for their fellow men. Can there be a greater aim in life?

Chapter 22:

Abilities Vary

Give the leading role in a film, stage play, or television drama to four quite different actors and each would perform the part in a totally individual way, bringing to the role those facets which they saw in the character they were playing. None would be wrong but clearly the director or producer would find one style more in keeping with the manner in which he personally saw the role being performed, albeit that each actor would be giving his own interpretation of the part he was being asked to play.

In Freemasonry experienced Preceptors are well aware of the target which they are striving to achieve and occasionally, very occasionally, they are blessed with an outstanding candidate who can and does carry out the roles assigned to him with a degree of perfection which both delights if not astounds brother Preceptor. In other words he brings to his role precisely the timing, pace and delivery which brother Preceptor has himself determined is ideal.

As sure as night follows day it is almost as certain that he has a brother in the same group whose abilities are as far in the other direction as it is possible to get. To combine the talents of two such brethren into a ceremony at the LOI without making the comparison between them quite obviously takes a man of quite exceptional ability.

How then should brother Preceptor set about this difficult if almost impossible task? He can of course use the less than able brother as a candidate, for that would immediately solve the problem and save embarrassment to all concerned. But he cannot do this every week, can he? The time will surely come when he has to face this dilemma and use both brethren together in a ceremony, possibly even working in unison.

At this point Brother Preceptor should remember just one fact which is so obvious that he might well overlook it if he is not careful. Both of the brethren we have described know their own capabilities as well as their own weaknesses and each will have his own private goals to attain. The first mentioned brother may be striving for a goal of which the Preceptor is not aware, it might be to perform a completely perfect second degree ceremony including the long tracing board, whilst the goal of the second brother might be to complete a given sentence without drying up or receiving a prompt. Each has his own target at which to aim and will not be influenced by the achievement or otherwise of his companion, therefore Brother Preceptor is worrying quite unnecessarily.

Strength frequently aids weakness and, from an experience covering many years, this author can recall several occasions where private tuition has been given by a more capable brother on a 'one to one' basis to a brother of limited ability and such has been the effect that two things happened.

First the level of ability of the weaker brother increased in leaps and bounds, and secondly that brethren of two quite separate abilities became firm friends as did their families by the simple process of one giving assistance to the other. Such was the friendship thus formed that on one occasion the two families spent their summer holidays together in France, for they found during their frequent weekly meetings that they had a conjoint interest in caravanning.

What then are the lessons to be learned from the scenario outlined above? Firstly that individuals are well aware of their own strengths and weaknesses and can handle them without feeling any embarrassment whatsoever. Secondly that a strength in one area invariably makes up for a weakness in another. Remember that your fears and concerns for given situations may not be mirrored by those for whom you have that concern.

For every Laurence Olivier there are thousands of competent actors each of whom is equally dedicated to his craft and will give of his best in everything he does. It is the few, the very few, who stand out like beacons on a dark night and who rise to the pinnacle of attainment. This does not demean in any way the efforts of the less headline-worthy supporting cast. For let us forget, if we dare, that even Laurence Olivier needed a supporting cast in every film he made and it was only by such support that he had the opportunity to let his outstanding ability shine through.

Finally we should ALWAYS remember that the brother has yet to be born who comes to a meeting of the lodge itself, or the Lodge of Instruction, intending to carry out his role badly. Each does the best he can with the faculties he has at his disposal. We know this has been said before in this book but it remains as true as ever.

It is perhaps a prophetic statement to make but experience in life will show that one strength usually makes up for a resultant weakness in another area which may not always be immediately obvious to the onlooker. The surgeon may not be able to mend an electrical fault in a cooker, the electrician may not be able to plough a straight furrow and the farmer may not be able to perform a surgical operation, but we need each and every one of them for their individual capabilities and what is more they all make up that great broad brush stroke of life called humanity.

Chapter 23:

Never Push Too Hard

We have to accept that in Freemasonry as in every facet of life we shall have to deal with those individuals who will be dedicated as well as those who show less than the level of enthusiasm which we ourselves would wish to see in an ideal member of our Lodge of Instruction.

What then can we do about such a member, for here we are looking at a brother who could, if he so tried, do considerably better than he is currently demonstrating? Given a task to perform for the following week he either does not arrive or, if he does, indicates he has not had the time to look at his book, or, if he participates, performs his role with an apparent laxity of effort and concern.

To begin to understand such a person we have to start from the standpoint that our own enthusiasm and dedication will not necessarily be mirrored by everyone with whom we come into contact in Freemasonry. We, as the Preceptor of the Lodge of Instruction, give up an evening every week to take this class of instruction year in and year out, and who but the most dedicated freemason would wish to accept such a role?

The answer to the lethargic member may appear to be simple. The brother concerned can be faced with his apparent lack of interest in a direct approach with a request to improve his performance, his dedication and his commitment.

The result is very likely to be a discontinuance of his membership of the Lodge of Instruction combined with a lack of interest in attending the meetings of the lodge for other than social reasons.

We have to accept that for every one of us who has a dedicated interest in the learning and performing of the ceremonies there will equally be another brother who will not wish (for whatever reason) to take such an involved and ongoing level of participation. This does not make such a brother a bad member or a lesser freemason as a result, it simply indicates that his interest in learning and performing the ritual is not as great as our own and nothing more. We should not under any circumstances consider him to be a lesser mortal as a result.

Such brethren can and do make excellent members of the lodge and also the LOI, frequently taking on the offices in the lodge of Almoner, Charity Steward, Organist or Assistant Secretary, all of which require a level of dedication if they are to be performed with advantage to the lodge.

Let us now turn to a totally different case where we have to make a subjective judgement about a brother who, although he attends the Lodge of Instruction on a regular basis and participates in the ceremonies to the best of his ability, clearly does not have the necessary level of achievement to progress through to the Master's chair. What can and should be done about such a brother, if anything at all?

The answer will depend entirely upon the brethren of the lodge and their attitude towards a brother who has tried very hard to progress in the learning of the ritual but has found the process extremely difficult if not impossible, but who from all other points of view is a first class member of the lodge.

He supports the charities and is always ready to carry out any job requested of him.

If the lodge membership (via its various Masters) so decide, he can be allowed to progress through the various offices, being given maximum support throughout, so that he eventually arrives at the Master's chair where he simply opens and closes the lodge, whilst other more capable Past Masters perform the ceremonies for him.

Is there anything wrong with such a decision if it is decided to enact it? What we have described in arriving at the above decision is Freemasonry in action in perhaps its most tangible form. Such a situation as described in the last paragraph above occurred recently in his mother lodge where a brother of 83 who had for sixteen years loyally served as the lodge Almoner, carrying out his duties with impeccable dedication and efficiency, travelling the length and breadth of the country attending to his various charges. He was placed in the chair of the Senior Warden and assisted to carry out his role by the strategic placing of a capable brother nearby.

During his year as Master the work of the lodge other than the opening and closing was undertaken by Past Masters and the installation of his successor was performed by the author, but allowing the Master to place the collar of his office around the neck of his successor and then place him in the chair of King Solomon.

This Master brought to the lodge year a totally different ambiance from any other that could be remembered for over forty years. Everyone including the visitors was aware that his Mastership was a reward for his dedication and service to the lodge over so many years. He was never short of assistance or assistants and by his willingness to accept such help he made others feel useful and necessary as well. He brought dignity to his role by not trying to hide his shortcomings in the performance of the ritual. He allowed everyone to realize he was not a skilled ritualist and that he needed their help to carry through his year as Master with efficiency. This was probably one of the happiest years many members could remember for a very long time.

The sting in the tail of this totally true story is that the same brother had been the Secretary at the Lodge of Instruction for well over twelve years and had never missed a single meeting, travelling right across London in the process throughout the cold winter months. Did the brethren do the right thing in voting him into the Master's chair? You decide.

Chapter 24:

Individual Instruction

Few things in this life are absolutely certain except for the one single fact that no matter how important we may believe we are to humanity we shall most certainly all expire one day.

One fact that comes very close to being equally as certain is that during your period of Preceptorship you will encounter a brother or brethren who require a greater degree of personal assistance than can ever be achieved at the weekly Lodge of Instruction.

How then do we recognize the necessity for such instruction and how can it best be dealt with? We are already giving one evening a week to the task of training the brethren of the lodge which in itself is an ongoing commitment, and we must after all give due consideration to the demands of our family.

Personal observation will show when a brother, despite frequent regular attendance at the Lodge of Instruction, simply does not improve and seems to be stuck in a rut from which he appears to be incapable of removing himself. Someone once said that 'the only difference between being stuck in a groove and being stuck in a rut was the height of the walls'!

Unless the problems of such a brother are recognized and dealt with in a caring and sympathetic manner you will almost certainly be faced with one of two situations.

The first is that the brother will become disappointed in his own lack of progress and cease his regular weekly attendance at the LOI. The second and worse still is that he will feel he cannot face the rest of the brethren who are all apparently managing to learn the ritual without any of the difficulties from which he suffers.

Therefore it is essential that any demonstrated strength is bolstered by you with a kindly word of encouragement for any achievement which you consider praiseworthy and there is always something if you look for it. For such a brother just a few lines can make the difference between success and failure and providing his difficulty is identified at an early stage you can give him a little 'homework' each week which need not be extensive in any sense. A paragraph or small piece of ritual which will be used at the LOI the following week can be the target at which to aim. Ensure that when you ask the brother so identified that you do so out of the hearing of the remainder of the brethren so that if he should not manage to achieve the desired goal it will not be public knowledge but simply a minor disappointment between the two of you.

To bring a brother back into regular attendance at the LOI or at the lodge itself once he has made the subjective decision to leave either entity, or simply make spasmodic or intermittent visits (albeit not resigning his membership) is a much more difficult matter and requires two hurdles to be cleared.

There is, however, a way in which this can be done and that is by asking the brother in writing to carry out a small task at the next meeting, albeit you might have 'manufactured' the reason for so asking. To carry out any task satisfactorily gives great pleasure to the brother carrying it out and if properly handled this can lead to a request to tackle another small part at the next meeting and so on.

This method will ensure two things, firstly that the brother will attend and secondly it will show that he still has enough interest to take on a task and carry it through to completion. It is always a very good idea to ensure that he receives the congratulations of other Past Masters on what he has achieved during a particular meeting.

The lesson we learn here is that if you keep a close eye on a problem as it becomes visible within your LOI you may well avoid having to take the second suggested course to redeem a situation which has moved too far away from you. Therefore do not just care for the members who are doing well or those who are coming up to their mastership in the next few years.

Those at the bottom of the lodge list of members are equally entitled to your close attention as those with whom you have been working for many years and, who knows, it could well be that at this stage in their membership they may need that encouragement more.

This writer has knowledge of personal Sunday morning instruction being given for an hour or so to a brother with particular learning difficulties. It was quickly discovered that the brother concerned did in fact suffer from a form of dyslexia and remedial action was instituted with the help of another brother who was a medical practitioner.

Sadly the brother suffering from this form of word blindness was in fact single and in his late twenties and had never been so diagnosed before, having always been considered at school to be 'below average'. Help in the form of an occupational therapist was subsequently forthcoming and within three months a remarkable transformation was already becoming evident. Twelve months on and the brother concerned was making progress at a pace that astounded his Preceptor and his fellow brethren alike. From a shy diffident unsure member a confident aspiring brother emerged. He met and married within three years and is now a happy married man with two delightful children.

Can Freemasonry claim to have achieved this success? Perhaps by recognizing a problem and aiding its solution it played its part. Therefore, Brother Preceptor, keep your eyes and ears open when going about your duties, for you never know in which form your help might be required or what you might discover when conducting 'one to one' individual instruction.

Chapter 25:

Working to a Plan

In chapter five we dealt with the annual plan of work and this heading may appear at first sight to be a duplication of the former chapter, but such is not the case, for here we are to deal with the individual rather than the composite learning plan.

A plan in the sense in which we are using the word on this occasion is a way of proceeding, a way in which we can bring along together at the same time brethren of differing abilities and differing learning curves and yet end with a sense of achievement at each level in which we operate.

Some brethren will operate best under pressure, by being given three or four pages of ritual to learn by the following week, for example. Others will progress far better if given just a few lines to learn in a month and then progress equally slowly to the next few lines. Every member of the Lodge of Instruction is an entirely separate entity motivated by quite different goals and desires. Getting to know what are those goals and desires, as related to their masonic interest, may well take a skilled Preceptor some months to determine, but determine it he should, for so much of the interest and progress of the individual will result from a clearly constructed programme of achievement designed especially for that member and for no one else.

This all sounds very complicated but it really is not if you think of your charges as falling into one of three groups. Let us call them for the sake of simplicity A, B and C. We shall take each group quite separately and illustrate the logic, pace, pressure and testing which should be applied to extract the maximum amount of satisfaction from the member himself as well as the progress in his masonic ability.

Group 'A'. In this group we shall place those bright, intensely keen and fast learning brethren whose ability is never in question from the first time they attend their initial meeting of the LOI.

The logic which has to be applied to this group is simple. We show them immediately that we are aware of their capabilities and have a plan already prepared for their progress through the various parts of the ritual they will be required to learn in their progress through to the Master's chair. We shall never doubt their ability to memorize a given passage or indeed be surprised when they exceed our expectations, for surely we expect nothing less, do we? On every occasion we should demonstrate our satisfaction with their progress but without the need to overstate the situation. Perhaps if the occasion should demand it we might express a slight amount of surprise when a given section has not been learned as well as we might have expected, without the need to criticize but with perhaps a small show of surprise.

The pace and pressure for this group has to be one of constant progress, for the members who constitute a rating for the 'A' group are not prepared to improve at the speed of the convoy. They are individualists and expect to be treated as such and you will stimulate their interest if you ensure that the pace for them is constant and perhaps just a little ahead of what they would ideally like to have as their target. This grouping constantly needs a challenge and with such a challenge in place they will progress at a surprisingly fast pace. Hold them back and their interest will wane.

Testing this group should be quite a severe matter. You should expect a minimum of eighty per cent accuracy from anything they do and as they progress this accuracy as related to work carried out before should improve to over ninety per cent. Accept nothing less for this is the group to whom anything short of complete success is unthinkable. If your testing of this group indicates that you are satisfied with a fifty per cent accuracy performance you will take away the winning post which so many in this group see as their goal in life in everything they do. The members who form this group, and they are rare, are the winners, the leaders, the successful people who have taken their schooling in their stride, their higher education has been a simple extension of their schooling and they have very probably achieved a level of some excellence in their university degree.

Underrate anyone in this group at your peril!

Group 'B'. Into this group will fall the eighty-five per cent of your charges who will in some cases need only modest support and in others considerable time and just occasionally a little private tuition to enable them to maintain their progress. The pressure and pace at which you direct the efforts of this group will be determined for you mainly because this is where the bulk of the 'convoy' will travel.

The logic to be applied here is that of carrot and stick, namely giving the encouragement which it is felt is necessary followed by a reward for effort or a rebuke for poor performance, not of course in any unkind way but perhaps by making it obvious that a performance has been less exacting than that which you had been expecting.

The pace and pressure for such brethren will need to be such that they will react in a positive way to such treatment and strive to prove their ability, especially if Brother Preceptor goes out of his way to show to a slow learning brother that he has your whole-hearted support in what he is trying to achieve. Task, reward, task, reward, and yet more tasks and more rewards. This method of achieving results is certainly time-proven and such individual tuition followed carefully will show to the student and to the instructor that by working together as a team they can achieve the desired results.

It can also show in the most tangible manner the way in which Brother Preceptor is prepared to help his charges. This is Freemasonry in action at its most basic level.

Testing should be fair and rewarding, perhaps even giving a little more praise than might at first sight be due to its recipient, for here we are trying to encourage our brethren who will undoubtedly feel and be unsure of their own ability and have less than complete confidence that they can and will eventually conquer this strange form of verbiage which they are required to digest by reason of the member-ship of the craft. As we said at the start of this section this grouping will occupy most of Brother Preceptor's time, for here reside the bulk of his seed-corn for the years which lie ahead.

Group 'C'. This group is where the stragglers find themselves. Many will, if not carefully nurtured, give up and not attend the LOI again. Any achievement, no matter how basic, will please the members of this group, for they are under-achievers and have been so for most of their lives. This is not to say that they do not have well-paid jobs or own businesses, or for that matter have happy and contented lives and families to match.

The logic which has to be applied to this group is important. They are for the most part people who have proceeded at their own pace in life not setting themselves very difficult targets to achieve and thereby have very probably never been 'stretched' in any respect mentally.

The reaction to learning by many in this group can be one of immediate rejection of both the thought and the intent of learning anything at all, either now or in the future.

Ask such a brother: "Can you repeat the Lord's prayer, the National Anthem or your favourite hymn or song?" For the most part the answer will most certainly be "yes" which will prove that they do have a learning facility even if they deny such a capability. Ask them how they learnt such things and the answer is almost certainly going to be "I do not know". In truth they have learned from the repetitious method of hearing the same thing again and again and again without even realizing that they have retained it in their brain. Proof of this can be found in the latest tune we hear continuously played on the radio or television.

On such a simple base can be built a worthwhile relationship by asking the brother concerned if he would be prepared to come along to the LOI for the next three weeks providing you guaranteed that he would not be required to participate in the proceedings but could simply sit and watch and listen to what occurred. You will rarely if ever get a refusal and his attendance will allow you to sit together and build a growing relationship and at the same time allow him to be comfortable in this new strange environment which was, until his first visit, totally unfamiliar to him.

Repeat the offer at the end of the first three weeks and invite him to attend for another three weeks—he will. Six weeks of regular association is certainly enough to bring two brethren together and at the end of that time you can extend the period if you feel it necessary for a further six weeks.

Eventually such a brother will volunteer to take a role in the order of things, albeit it might only be that of a candidate but he will participate. There are few people in this life who given the chance will not wish to 'belong' in all senses of the word. Belonging to the group, belonging to the herd, belonging to an organization in which they recognize people whom they will wish to emulate. The commitment here is to get a regular attendance from this point onwards and then as the Chinese would say 'make haste slowly'.

Testing anyone in this group should be handled with very great care indeed. We are clearly in the business of building confidence in our charges, not destroying them, therefore it is always (with this grouping) essential that we compliment whenever we can, that we praise whenever we can, that we encourage and enthuse whenever we can. The brethren in this group need to believe in themselves and you are the one person, Brother Preceptor, who can make that dream come true.

You are caring for the equivalent of a valuable hybrid plant at this stage of a brother's masonic career. Nurture it with care, love and attention as you would a valuable prize-winning exhibit and the return on your devotion and hard work will be repaid many times over.

Chapter 26:

How Not To Get Results

This chapter has been included to show in definitive form just how the way in which Brother Preceptor approaches his role can have entirely the wrong effect upon the Lodge of Instruction. To illustrate how this can and does happen, a number of examples are given from which it will be seen that there are many facets to the art of teaching, some of them laden with potential time bombs.

The Dictator

Let us take as our first example the dictator. This is a brother who is clearly very knowledgeable where masonic ritual is concerned. He is also equally skilled in delivering it in the Lodge of Instruction and never hesitates for one moment to show just how available that skill is by stepping in and delivering large pieces of whatever ritual is being practised every time a nervous, unsure member looks as though he might be going to falter in his delivery.

This type of Preceptor carries out the exact opposite of the task he is there to fulfil. Instead of taking an unsure candidate metaphorically by the hand and leading him gently through the more complicated parts of the ritual, thus bolstering his confidence and making him feel he has achieved a degree of competence, by words of encouragement together with the odd whispered word of assistance when necessary, he only succeeds in depressing him.

He does in fact manage to accomplish exactly the opposite by showing the candidate just how much he does NOT know and moreover emphasizes the depth of his lack of knowledge by demonstrating in front of everyone how much more he has to learn before he can be considered to have made any progress whatsoever. Brother

Preceptor should always remember that he is there to build confidence, NOT destroy it.

Brother Preceptor NEVER has a need to prove his competency in ritual delivery to the members of the LOI on any occasion whatsoever. There is never an exception to this rule.

A Preceptor holds his office by virtue of his service to the lodge which has been proved over many years, most if not all of them carried out with diligence and dedication long before any of the current members of the LOI had been initiated into the craft.

He will automatically be regarded as the 'ultimate authority' by those who attend that LOI, for after all he is the head of this teaching institution and anything he imparts to his charges will be received instantly as though it were 'holy writ'.

Questions as to why we do this or that will undoubtedly come his way but his replies will never be questioned, indeed they will be accepted as both accurate and official. He must therefore make certain that they are.

To behave in the manner of a dictator is to alienate the members of the LOI, many of whom will probably hold positions of responsibility in their business lives and will not be prepared to accept being spoken to and generally treated in such a high-handed and unnecessary manner.

The most likely result will be that the persons so offended never attend the LOI (and possibly the lodge) again. The moral of this 'tale' of one type of Preceptor is that dictators within Lodges of Instruction seldome impress anyone except themselves. Usually they prove to those with whom they come into contact that they are in fact insecure individuals who have a considerable inferiority complex and have only this outlet through which to prove to themselves that they are not inferior and thus they vastly over-compensate as a result.

So do not be a dictator, be a persuasive helpful friend to whom all will turn for advice and who will use your friendly shoulder to lean on when things do not go exactly the way they wish, and we all have a day like that, do we not?

Mr Nice Guy

This Preceptor wants, indeed needs, to be liked, in fact the need to be liked is far more important to him than that his charges should gain anything from the class he supervises each week. He over-compensates on every occasion and he gives praise to everyone about everything, no matter how they carry out their respective duties.

He allows interruptions from the members during ceremony rehearsals and allows prompts from other members without correcting their behaviour. He allows members to have their ritual books open throughout the meeting and generally lacks any form of authority or for that matter respect.

The members will agree, no doubt, that the Preceptor is a 'nice guy', but when such brethren are privately asked they usually admit that they would like to see someone with a stronger control who would lead from the front and strive for better performances and also insist on a better quality of meeting overall.

Being fair and maintaining control will produce a better Lodge of Instruction meeting. Knowing that personal praise only comes when an outstanding performance has been witnessed means that the praise thus given is rated more highly by the brother receiving it, whereas if everyone is praised every week about everything there really is little value in it.

The moral here is simple, being 'The Nice Guy' is all very well but you were appointed to obtain results with the co-operation of the brethren who have been placed in your care, not to win a popularity contest. You therefore owe it to the lodge members to carry out your duties for the benefit of all the members and not so that you personally will end up being the most popular man in the lodge.

Being liked and being respected are two completely different things. Of course it is nice to be liked but it's far more beneficial to your lodge that you are respected for carrying out a difficult job with ability and dedication and that your members once trained perform their work in the lodge to the satisfaction of the Master who appointed them and with pleasure to themselves at having achieved a degree of competency which perhaps they never expected.

It is very easy to fall into this grouping, for we all have a deep rooted and fundamental desire to be liked, just make sure it does not happen to you.

Mr Know It All

This is a quite different type of Preceptor from the Dictator mentioned at the beginning of this chapter. This Preceptor runs an efficient Lodge of Instruction. He balances his praise and his correction of members with scrupulous fairness and has a very happy group of members and a successful record of achievement with those who have passed through its portals over the years. This brother has one great failing. It is that no matter what question he may be asked on any masonic subject no matter how obtuse he ALWAYS has an answer. It may be correct, accurate or simply arrived at by deduced logic, but he has to give an answer on the spot with the assurance that every feature and facet of his reply is so accurate and certain that it should never be questioned under any circumstances.

There are very few brethren of this author's experience who would fall into such a category. Indeed the combined talents of the members of the Quatuor Coronati Lodge No 2076, the Premier Lodge of Masonic Research in the world, would steer very clear of giving total and complete answers to any and every question thrown at them.

Freemasonry has so many diverse and tangented aspects that for many of the questions which Brother Preceptor may be asked there are no certain or absolute answers, simply opinions based on the only knowledge we have at this time backed by such facts as may be available. Ongoing masonic research continues to correct many of our long held beliefs and will probably do so for centuries to come.

It therefore necessarily follows that Brother Preceptor cannot possibly have an accurate and precise answer to every single question he is asked by his members and how much better and indeed more human for him to reply if only occasionally "I really do not know the answer to that question but I will endeavour to find the answer for you and tell you next week what my research has produced". His stock will rise in the LOI, for we all appreciate an individual who says he does not know something but will try to find out, do we not?

The moral here is easy to discern. A man who knows everything about everything is a bore and will quickly earn for himself a reputation as a 'Mr Know It All'. The trouble with this title is that in actual fact the vast majority of the people to whom he speaks do not believe a single word he says, so far from being a fountain of all knowledge he ends up being the epitome of everything that is undesirable and questionable. Do not be a 'Mr Know It All', it really does not work.

The Shy Retiring Type

This Preceptor is usually a knowledgeable, quietly confident member of the lodge who for a variety of reasons finds himself being the ONLY brother prepared to take on the role of teaching the brethren the nuances of the rituals we use. He could very well be a 'backroom boy' in some organization or other who has never before had to take centre stage and organize and run anything in his life.

His year in office as Master of the lodge was probably the first occasion that he ever had to address a meeting. His period in that role will have been one of quiet competence which proved to his fellow brethren his ability to learn, remember and recite the ritual. He most decidedly is not an extrovert in any sense of the word, in fact in many cases he will be quite the opposite, introvert in virtually everything he undertakes, a state of mind with which he has been and is completely happy and has no intention of changing.

How then did this brother find himself controlling a group of brethren all of whom were looking to him for a form of leadership, something for which he had never been trained nor prepared and indeed did not wish to undertake?

It might well be the case that distance from the LOI meeting place prevented a more suitable brother from taking on this role or that there simply was no one else prepared to accept the position when it fell vacant.

We therefore have a situation where a shy, perhaps reticent, brother is at the head of what is the most important educational establishment that any lodge has with which to secure its continuity.

Such a brother has a wealth of opportunities at his disposal, for he is already known as a 'quiet type' by the brethren whom he is there to instruct. He will also be known for his competence in everything he does in the lodge and his credentials are therefore known in advance.

He can combine his natural reticence and shyness and use them to the advantage of the LOI by setting an atmosphere from the first day he is in charge of his new responsibility. The members will quickly understand and appreciate their new Preceptor's personality and out of a sense of kindness will wish to help this shy brother in his new role. Such retiring brethren as we have described are universally liked, for we all have a sense of protection within our beating breasts and such people bring out of us the desire to protect, nurture and assist them. That is strange but true.

Surprisingly enough this brother can fail if he tries to be something he is not. If he decides that his natural retiring personality will inhibit his new role and thereby also decides to put on 'metaphorically speaking' an overcoat of confidence, how sad this will be for this never works. It sounds false and it looks false because of course that is what it is.

The moral here is simple. Never try to be what you are not, be appreciated for what you are and what you do. It is surprising just how much people like and value genuine sincerity. An honest man doing his best in an unfamiliar situation will usually find that he is backed to the hilt provided he does not try to be something he is not.

Chapter 27:

Playing the Waiting Game

The following scenario will sometimes occur and perhaps a true story of one way to handle such a situation to advantage will assist Brother Preceptor should he ever find himself in a similar situation.

A young man in his early twenties is admitted a member of the lodge and after completing his three degrees is encouraged to attend the LOI. He does so and quickly finds that there is considerably more to learn than perhaps he has ever thought would be the case, if indeed he has ever thought about it at all. We should say right away that any candidate for our order should be properly briefed about his forthcoming responsibilities, but in truth can one really explain to a potential new member just what the learning process will consist of without perhaps scaring off what might well be a useful addition to the lodge and to freemasonry?

Such a situation occurred during the writer's ten-year period of Preceptorship (when he was Secretary of his lodge). A bright young man in his early twenties who was a police officer told the writer he felt that perhaps he had made a mistake in joining the lodge. He simply did not have the time to attend each week and as he had many years of study before him in his career he did not feel he could be the sort of member of the lodge which his proposer and seconder would wish and therefore he should, out of consideration for the lodge, resign forthwith.

The Secretary wrote to him at some length, telling him that his prime duty was to attend to his private studies and so render the future secure for himself and his family and that he should complete this process before he attempted to progress in the lodge. He stated further that no one would think any the less of him whilst he studied, sat and hopefully passed his examinations in his chosen profession.

The advice was accepted and the young man took and quickly passed his Sergeants' examination and with two short years thereafter was made an Inspector. Subsequently he was seconded to the police training college at Bramshill from where he emerged some three years later as a Chief Inspector. He later progressed to Superintendent, then Chief Superintendent, and now holds the rank of Commander whilst still in his mid-forties.

Once through his Inspectors' examination and with his hardest study behind him, but with a brain which had been dedicated to study and learning for a number of years, he started to read and practice the ritual used by his lodge. As a result he became one of the finest Masters the lodge had experienced for many years. He has now completed a two-year period in charge of his mother Chapter and thoroughly enjoyed the experience, performing the ceremony with considerable ability and assurance. We now have an experienced lodge and chapter officer still under fifty with many years to serve in any office to which he is appointed.

This is a true story told without any exaggeration whatsoever.

The moral here is very clear. Push a young man too hard whilst he has his mind set on making his way in the world and you could well lose a first class Master of ten years hence.

Be far sighted with your planning and care for the whole member, not just his masonic attendance, and you will not only produce a good lodge officer and eventually a first class Master but you will have also made a firm friend for life.

The other and perhaps most important message you will also have communicated is that Freemasonry cares about its members, their families and their future.

A Preceptor who gets to know his members well by understanding those things which motivate them and those mountains they have to climb, metaphorically speaking, will be dealing with the whole man and not just that part of him which appears on masonic occasions.

Remember that we all have many facets to our lives involving many different emotions which can and do motivate us. Without wishing to turn every Preceptor into a clinical psychologist, the more we can stand back a little and look at what is best for the 'whole' man rather than that part we wish to see serve our needs in the lodge, the happier will be our lodge as well as the member about whom we have thought deeply.

Freemasonry cares about its members, their families and their dependants and it hurts not at all to let the whole world be aware of this basic and fundamental fact about our order.

Chapter 28:

Making Friends for Life

It is doubtful if there is one freemason in the craft today who cannot remember with crystal clarity the Preceptor or Preceptors of his Lodge of Instruction, together with the nuances which they used, their gentle or harsh methods of explanation and training and their friendly word of help when things clearly were not going as well as the brother under training had hoped.

It is perhaps unnecessary and even trite to remind the reader that freemasons come from every type of background. Educational ability and strength in one sphere is in no way an automatic guarantee for success in ritual ability or performance. Such perfection, if indeed perfection it is, comes from dedication in reading, regular rehearsal, and generally absorbing what is after all a totally new style or type of language for the vast majority of those embarking on their masonic careers. It really is quite surprising how often from a level start those enthusiastic brethren who truly dedicate themselves can and will make giant strides in progress and ritual retention.

One such example is told principally because it is quite true but more so because it had side effects which no one including this Preceptor ever thought possible. A candidate for initiation came before the Committee of Management for interview regarding his admission into the lodge.

During the interview he demonstrated that he had a stutter of considerable proportions, which clearly embarrassed him. This stutter became much worse when responding to questions put by the dozen or so members of the committee. Naturally this difficulty was mentioned during the ensuing discussion relative to his ever being able to hold office. The candidate met the basic rules for admission into our order and was subsequently initiated and thereby became a member of the lodge.

Subsequent discussion ensued after he had been raised and his entry to the LOI became imminent. What if anything could this brother achieve? Would he and perhaps the brethren be embarrassed by his pronounced stutter which on occasions reduced him almost to a 'non-speaking jelly'?

The Preceptor invited this newly raised brother to join him the following week and placed him in a seat next to himself, explaining the various sections of the ceremony under rehearsal. This continued for many weeks without the new entrant making any attempt or indeed being invited to fill an office, albeit he tried to give the VSL closing ritual and had great difficulty.

This Preceptor gradually got to know the new brother on a one to one basis and after a number of weeks was invited by his new recruit to 'come home for coffee' one evening after the LOI finished.

Almost immediately he was inside his own front door the stutter all but disappeared and within the portals of his own home he was, speech-wise, a very different man from the one who had been struggling with just a small passage at the LOI an hour earlier.

We tried a private experiment without telling the rest of the members of the LOI. This was a simple but effective part answer to his problem. We asked the brother to take a view of his living room in his mind and when he had a portion of ritual to deliver to close his eyes, bring the vision of his living room into his mind and deliver the ritual. Within two or three weeks everyone but everyone was making comments on his progress, such comments as 'his stutter has all but disappeared'.

Could he ever make a competent lodge officer? Subjective views were aired and eventually with some obvious relief by all concerned it was decided to 'leave the situation in the hands of the Preceptor' to advise the Master of the year whether or not he thought Bro —— would be able to carry out the offices without causing embarrassment to himself or disrupting the dignity which we try to maintain in all the ceremonies we carry out.

Without wishing to prolong this story let us come to the end result, which was surprising to everyone of his fellow brethren.

The brother concerned quickly made progress simply because he had proved to himself that he was capable of learning the ritual.

What was more he recited it back with considerable ability and with only the very occasional slight stutter which could generally be related to the small amount of stress which he was undergoing at that moment. Thus it had been determined quite clearly that his stutter was stress-related.

His overall ability to speak without stuttering amongst his family and friends improved immeasurably. He went on to become a useful member of his local community by serving on his local council and eventually becoming the Chairman of a sub-committee which meant many speeches and control of meetings, something he would never have dreamed of when he joined the lodge.

The moral here is obvious. The brother of whom we write had gained confidence in his own ability by the simple lesson of getting him to feel relaxed and comfortable. The answer to his problem had been within his own home all the time, for there he felt secure, totally relaxed and comfortable and when he experienced all those emotions he did not stutter.

It is amazing, is it not, how often the answers to our problems are sometimes staring us in the face but we do not see them until someone else points them out? This author likes to feel that this brother's relationship with his brethren in Freemasonry gave him a better involvement in life generally than perhaps might otherwise have been the case.

The spin-off is that this brother although now many years past the chair has never forgotten the help and advice he was given in his earliest days in Freemasonry by 'his' lodge and 'his' Preceptor of whom he has made a friend for life.

Oh! and by the way the Preceptor learned something too!

Chapter 29:

Changing Your Venue

Most lodges hold their regular weekly Lodge of Instruction meetings in a secure venue and one which has probably been their regular meeting place or home for many years. To hold the regular rehearsals in a masonic hall is of course the ideal arrangement but this sadly cannot be the case with every lodge, particularly those situated in the London area. It is therefore necessary for some Lodges of Instruction to seek new or alternative premises often without much prior notice.

Many such meetings are held above licensed premises which can sometimes provide problems for the requirements of the members in two aspects. It will occasionally happen that a change of owner or management will result in the incoming licensee being anti-masonic in attitude or perhaps wishing to use the present LOI room for some other purpose and the members therefore find themselves looking for a new home.

Before proceeding further we would suggest to Brother Preceptor that if the requirement to move from one venue to another should occur then he would be well advised to read Rule 133 of the *Book of Constitutions* which covers the question of approval of such venues. Many Preceptors are not aware that such venues must be approved by the supervising authority, be that Grand Lodge or a Provincial or District Grand Lodge.

Such approval will usually be granted if the intended venue meets certain criteria amongst which are security, lockable doors, audibility control, accessibility and fire precautions being vitally important ingredients.

The secure storage of regalia is of course another important factor as is the facility to ensure that the room cannot be overlooked or viewed from outside the building in which the Lodge of Instruction is being held.

Venues vary considerably in their type, situation and facilities and it is very easy for the members of a Lodge of Instruction to believe that it rests with them to decide where and when they should meet and that they can change their venue without reference to anyone. Such, however, is not the case as will be clarified by the reading of Rules 132 and 133 of the *Book of Constitutions*.

All Lodges of Instruction are held under the auspices of the Lodge itself and the venue, timings of meetings and general management of the LOI are subject to the approval of higher authority. It is very often the case that the members of the LOI are advised (albeit wrongly) that they can make all such decisions without any reference to the Lodge itself. Another small but important fact which is sometimes not appreciated by both the members of the Lodge, as well as the members of the LOI, is that financially the costs incurred by the LOI if not met by that unit will fall upon the Lodge itself since this is the sponsoring body and the place where the final responsibility rests.

Do please remember that if a change of venue is to take place and also if there should be a change in the day of the week on which the LOI is held, then that fact must be reported to three groups.

Firstly, the Province or District under which the Lodge itself operates or, in the case of London, the Grand Secretary. Secondly the Lodge itself. Thirdly the membership of the LOI.

The first meeting of the LOI in its new abode MUST NOT be held until approval has been received from the supervising authority so please do not go ahead without that approval for you risk the wrath of 'those from above'.

Do make sure that the details of your new location are communicated to the Lodge Secretary in order that it may appear on the next Lodge summons and also that it may be minuted at the next lodge meeting. Thus any future query regarding your move of the LOI which may come 'from above' can be answered without difficulty.

Remember also those members who attend only occasionally and ensure that they do not arrive at the previous venue only to find that you have 'moved' and have failed to notify them.

Lastly and most importantly please remember that where a Lodge of Instruction meets in a location which is other than a masonic hall, there is an ongoing need to ensure that all conversation and behaviour is carefully controlled, for we must at all times remember that we are ambassadors for the craft in everything we do when communicating with the 'uninitiated or popular world who are not freemasons'!

Chapter 30:

Your Retirement

The day will surely dawn when, through design, age, infirmity or perhaps even the feeling that the time is right, you will wish to retire from your role as the Head of the Lodge Educational system, for that is surely what the Preceptor of the Lodge of Instruction should be called.

It is never a bad thing to start your period of office as the Preceptor of the Lodge of Instruction with a fixed time-frame for your retirement from that office which is known well in advance to all concerned. This may sound rather a strange statement to make and perhaps even seem to indicate that you are not fully committed to the role to which you have just been elected but this is most certainly not the case as will be demonstrated.

There is occasionally a period during one's term of office when the role being held changes from one of devout enthusiasm and dedication to one of 'if only I didn't have to go to the LOI this evening'. The demands of the weekly class of instruction upon the dedicated Preceptor are constant and ongoing and can scarcely be appreciated by the average member of that school of training. Members come and members go usually after occupying the Master's chair and then they quietly cease to attend as regularly as once was the case. Other new members take their places, anxious to increase their proficiency in the ritual and get all the assistance they can from the Preceptor as they pass through the offices leading up to the Master's chair.

Seldom if ever do the members of the LOI think about the dedication which the Preceptor gives to his duties. He is always there, helping, coaxing, offering the kind word and occasionally, very occasionally, giving a metaphorical smack on the wrist to the brother who has clearly not carried out his allotted task as well as he is able to do, and indeed has shown in the past what he could do.

Therefore to have a final finishing post in view is no bad thing. It allows the newly appointed Preceptor to be aware at the start of his period of office just how long his Preceptorship will last and then a plan can be formalized for a smooth transition to his successor. A short period of duality of Preceptors is sometimes a great asset for the Lodge at such a time and for the current Preceptor to have a Deputy officially appointed can allow him to enjoy the occasional week away from his regular responsibility.

Brother Preceptor should make his intentions clear to the members of the Lodge well in advance of his retirement from office and a full twelve-month period is by no means too great a period of time to have in mind.

The converse of this statement is for the brother who has guided the Lodge of Instruction through many years of learning suddenly to be no longer available for whatever reason and for the LOI to enter a period of instability by 'making do' with stand-in Preceptors until a permanent appointment can be made.

This can result in the wrong person being talked into accepting the appointment, mainly because there is no one else prepared to carry out the role. Such a bad change at the top of the learning academy can and frequently does have 'knock on' effects for the 'old' Preceptor knew his charges well and he was aware of just how far he could gently 'push' a brother and who should never be asked to try and do too much.

An incoming brother without experience, albeit that he is a skilled Past Master, has himself a learning curve to accomplish before he can truthfully be said to be 'in charge'. It can take a new man a full masonic season to get to grips with the abilities and shortcomings of his members. This is a testing time for a new Preceptor, for comparisons can and will be made between him and his predecessor, not all of which will be favourable, for we all have our own individual mannerisms, annoying habits and general beliefs plus likes and dislikes.

Remember if you will that in chapter four we talked about the first impression gained by the 'new' member to the LOI and how we all experience a range of emotions when first introduced into a new situation. The same factors apply to people. We all, sometimes without knowing it, sum up the person to whom we are being introduced and place that person into a category in our mind. A newly introduced brother entering his LOI meets for the first time in his life a Preceptor. This is the person against whom all other Preceptors for the rest of his masonic life will be judged.

Ergo the replacement Preceptor who is taking over the LOI from his highly successful predecessor has a number of factors with which to contend, not the least of which is his popularity.

The moral here is to tread gently, listen carefully and speak with care, for you are under as much scrutiny as that with which you are scrutinizing your new charges, perhaps even more.

Beauty it is said is in the eye of the beholder—perhaps the LOI member sees something in the new Preceptor which the new Preceptor does not see in the LOI member?

Chapter 31:

And Finally

Many words, much advice, plenty of mention of actual experiences, all are contained in the pages of this book. Can the reading of such a publication make a Preceptor out of an inexperienced but enthusiastic Past Master? The answer to this question must surely depend upon the individual, for some will read, learn and inwardly digest and apply the suggestions and words of advice with advantage to the membership. Others will read, disagree, discard and do it their own way.

Such are the foibles of human beings that advice, no matter how well intentioned, is frequently ignored, put to one side, or totally disregarded. How then can this book help you in your future work at the LOI?

This book was designed to cover as many of the facets which occur in the running of a lodge as the author could possibly muster. It is not suggested or indeed guaranteed that every single issue upon which the new Preceptor will need guidance is covered in these pages, but it can certainly be stated that the majority of the problems and situations which the new Preceptor will encounter can be dealt with by reference to one chapter or another of this book.

Many Masters will be only too pleased to admit that without the Preceptor of their LOI they would never have progressed through to the chair of King Solomon and enjoyed the highest office the lodge has in its power to confer.

The author therefore dedicates this book to all those Preceptors both present and past as well as those to come whose weekly devotion year upon year has brought confidence to the shy and retiring, instilled enthusiasm where perhaps it was lacking, perfected the shortcomings of the unsure and polished and perfected many Masters for their year in the chair.

May your work bring you as much pleasure as it brought me over ten continuous years in the building, shaping and contouring a group of brethren whose backgrounds were as diverse as it was possible to imagine but who, by working together, perfected a team of unimaginable quality and smooth capability. May you have as much happiness in your work as I had in mine.

Oh! and by the way, have fun doing it, won't you?